Raised By a
Nine-year Old King: Vol 1

T0159138

Raised By a
Nine-year Old King: Vol 1

Hezekiah Nevels

authorHOUSE®

AuthorHouse™
1663 Liberty Drive
Bloomington, IN 47403
www.authorhouse.com
Phone: 1-800-839-8640

First published by AuthorHouse   08/23/2011

ISBN: 978-1-4634-0273-0 (sc)
ISBN: 978-1-4634-0269-3 (ebk)

Library of Congress Control Number: 2011907124

Printed in the United States of America

Any people depicted in stock imagery provided by Thinkstock are models, and such images are being used for illustrative purposes only.
Certain stock imagery © Thinkstock.

This book is printed on acid-free paper.

This story is about a nine year old boy given the opportunity to live on the streets of Philadelphia. He had to grow up through the most chaotic times in the history of America. Jim crow, Vietnam War, Gang Wars, Four assignations (John F. Kennedy Jr., Martin L. King Jr., Bobby Kennedy and Malcolm X), (Civil Rights Movement) Race riots, the Love and Peace movement (Sex and Drugs Revolution) and Motown and Rock & Roll (Music revolution). There were a lot of grown ups who did not survive those times. It's very interesting how this nine year old found his way through forty something years of fear, horror, torture, sex, drugs, people, places and things. Though the grace of GOD he made it.

By Hezekiah Nevels

This book is dedicated to three very special people in my life:
My Mother, the one who was the foundation of my love and forgiveness.

My sister, the one who was my boldness and sense of humor
And
My nephew, the one who gave me the vision of maturity and manhood.

I beg GOD, may they all rest in peace

INTRODUCTION

This is the first book of a five part series. Series number one "Raised by a Nine Year Old (King)". The four other series are not titled as of yet. Please understand that this book was written with a lot of emotion.

What I went through to get the words out was so devastating. It took a lot out of me, to recall those moments of time. I literally had to relive those moments of pain, horror, fear and torture. Some of those times were not as bad as others, but it was hard to do, just the same.

This first book is about a boy caught up in time. A time he never under stood. This boy was pushed to grow-up at time in his life, when he had no understanding of what he was about to go through. Everything came fast, untimed and shocking. He was shot out into life with no warning and no skills. He had to learn by trail and era. He is still carrying those traits with him today after over forty years.

He grew up and became a man, with the absence of that little boy, who never got a chance to experience what it would have been like to be one. He was always forcing himself to go through the elements of life, always fighting, hoping and praying. Today I can say he survived by the skin of his teeth.

The interesting thing about his survival is what, who, and how he went through these forty something years. In the series to come, you will learn about how he evolved, through those trying years.

This boy lived a life, that proves, that, when you are walking in the sand and one moment you look down and see two pairs of foot prints in the sand and for forty years of walking in that sand you only see one pair of foot prints. You know that you were carried through all those years. For that I am surely blesses. I know that I could not have walked through those forty years on my own. I stated earlier this boy had no warning and no skills.

Thank GOD for GOD

CHAPTER 1

The Train Ride

It was the year 1960, when I remember riding on this train at the early age of three going on four years old; we were leaving my hometown Lincoln Nebraska the town where I was born. I remember running up the else of the train and my mother shouting at me to stay in my seat. At that time in my life I was that high-energy child that was just happy without a care in the world. All I knew, at that time, was to have fun and play. She said that I could not keep, my underwear up, they always were falling down. I felt free to be me at that time in my life. I was not even knee high to a grasshopper but life was good. I did not know exactly what good, was, at that time but I learned real fast.

My mother was a fine looking young girl at that time traveling to a new city with five young children. Her intentions were to meet up with a young man that she was intending to marry. She met him in her hometown of Omaha Nebraska. He was in the army and they met one weekend when he was on leave. They hit it off great. She used to tell us how charming he was.

So they dated and they decided that when he was relived from duty she would bring her five children to the big city of brotherly love, (Philadelphia, Penn.) which is where he lived, to get married. I use to wonder why she divorced my father. He was fun and I loved him. But at that age I did not really care because I really did not know what was going on. In those days kids were told to go play and stay out of grown folk conversations. So that's why I was on that train at the early age of four, running up and down the else. I was having the time of my life. The train was old but we had food to eat and other goodies.

My name is Kevin. I was the fourth child. I had an older brother James, who was eight years old, and two older sisters June and Jennifer, June was six and Jennifer five. And then my younger sister Joanne she was two going on three year old and my youngest Sister Ann was one year old. Oh yea I said that my mother was a young girl and she was only twenty-two at that time. So yes she was a young girl. As we traveled from state to state I remember having a lot of fun. Not knowing that it was going to be a long time before, I have anywhere near that kind of fun again. I guess I remember so well because it was the only time in my life, when there was not any trauma or drama.

We all had so much fun together, my brother always played with me rolling are cars up and down the else, we didn't get into any mistrif or anything like that but we seamed to always be in some kind of trouble. My mother was young but she had some old fashion ways. She did not play when it came to punishing us. All she had to do was give us a certain look, and we new to stop doing what ever it was that we were doing. She used to tell us that she had a stern grandmother who did not let her get away with anything. And she would get beat every time that she did something wrong. On the average we were some good mannered children. I know now that all the toughness that my great grandmother put on her; she must have known what tough roads were up ahead for my mother. I believe her grandmother was getting her prepared for the road she was about to travel.

We were looking forward to our new place to live, even though we did not know what my mother was doing and why. She seamed to be very happy about the move. She wanted to get away from a boring country life and see what it was like in the big city. She was an adventurer; believe me she did get one too, that lasted for the rest of her life. A real adventure is what she got.

Everything was going fine as we traveled. We looked at all the different scenery through the windows and we even saw all types of animals. My brother and I had a great time playing together we even made time for our sisters, because they always wanted to do what we did. We were very close and never really had a lot of fights and things like that. It seam that we just didn't go through a lot changes in those days. Everything was happy go lucky. The day the train was pulling into the station we were all getting ourselves together to really meet this guy? It was a very cold day. It had just stopped snowing. We were dressed in our Sunday best and looking like new children. My mother would tell us how to be on our best behavior and mind our manners. She would talk so much about him. He had already been discharge from the service weeks earlier. He was waiting for her to come to the city with all of us. He was supposed to have had everything together for us.

We heard the conductor shout out "Thirtieth Street Station ". We all got off the train and stood on the platform; everybody was getting off or getting on the train. After everyone was aboard the train it began to pull off, going to its next station. He was not at the station when we got there. We had to wait for him to come. We were waiting a very long time, it began to turn night and we were tired. My mother continued to wait for him. As it got later and later we were hungry. He still has not shown up.

My mother had us on the benches all lay out. It got real late and very cold outside and my mother did not know what to do, she was stuck and stranded. Then out of nowhere this cab driver came up to her and said woman what are you doing out here with these babies. He said I couldn't stand around and see these babies cold and hungry. Please come with me so that my wife can feed these babies. So my mother went with him. Something in her spirit said go with this man. He took us to his home and fed us and let us sleep until the morning came. He gave my mother some more food to take with us. He asked her where did she want to go and she said take me back to the train station. That is just what he did. My mother thanked him and he told her that she was much welcomed. He dropped us back at the train station. My stepfather eventually he showed up. My mother asked him why did he take so long and he said that he got all caught up with getting things together for us. We eventually found out that he was just lying to her.

One thing he did have planned was the wedding ceremony at the justice of the peace. We left the train station and went to the City Hall building down town Philadelphia. All six of us were just following along as if we knew where we were going. We just were following him all happy and gay.

So we get to the City Hall building and go to the office of the justice of the peace. They filled out the necessary paper work and we all got in line and had to wait our turn.

We finally got our turn with the justice of the peace. They go through the ceremony and every thing is going fine until the end. I always felt that, at that time that was the real beginning of a time in our life.

As the Justice of the peace stated to this man that he could kiss the bride, instead of kissing her he said "Bitch you are mine now so get those little mother fuckers and lets get the fuck out of here." We all looked at each other, then we look at him and then we looked at my mother. We saw some looks that none of us have ever seen before. The looks were so puzzling, confusing and defiantly scary. At that time I had an inner filling that told me that we were about to meet the devil himself. The scary part about it was that the look I saw on everybody's face was the same. The crazy part about it was that I didn't even know anything about any devil. I just knew that what he just said was not right and it was not the language I ever heard. And it did not feel good at all. We ended up leaving with him and he took us to where we were supposed to live. I never had seen anything like it. He took us to the worst part of the city at that time (North Philadelphia) I cannot even remember what street it was on and I will never ask my mother ether.

On our way there I can remember seeing people smelling bad and look like street bums and junkies. The people didn't look anything like the people we were used to seeing. The so call place that he said was for us is almost indescribable. It was a one-room shack with a potbelly stove in the middle of the room. It had no furniture and it had a dirt floor. All six of us stayed in that shack with him his mother, (Martha), his brother (Jake), his brother's girlfriend, his mother's friend (Ronald), his mother's other friend (Harry) and they had two other fiends that we didn't know their names. There were thirteen people in one room. We also had an outhouse in the back somewhere. How we all lived in that shack at the same time I really do not remember. We found out that things were not going to be anything like what we were used to. As a matter of fact we knew that things were going to be different for a long time. There was one thing that convinced us that things were not going to get any better, it was when my mother, being the outspoken woman that she is, stood up for us on how he was talking to her and to her children. She was not having it. We were proud of her for standing up for us because she didn't take anybody stuff. Well after we helped pick her up off the floor with a swollen jaw. We did not want her to stand up for us again. The fear that came across her face changed the way she approached things after that.

We still were proud of her but we didn't want her to stand up no more. I knew she had to remember that she did not know anyone in Philly and she was far way from her hometown, and she didn't know anyone and he seem to know everybody. So I believe that she had to get into the protection mold. She had to look out for her five children and she had one on the way. This one was his. It was at that time, when I started to fell like a soldier in the army. My whole body began to stiffen up and I began to ball up my fist and I did not know why. I also saw that same look in my brother's eyes. We knew that we had to lookout and even protect our mother and sisters. How we were going to do it was another question.

CHAPTER 2

We Declare War

My demeanor began to change. I became more serious as a child and the change came over me almost instantly. I began to fell like the war was on now. From that day on it seemed like we were fighting. That man beat everyone in the house, if we had a dog I'm sure he would have beat the dog too. He began to beat my mother on a regular basis. Every day she was getting beat for something. The first couple of times my brother and I would jump in to stop him. It always ended in us getting beat down. My mother told us to stop jumping in before he really hurt us bad. She just didn't know that we were already getting beat down and very badly. But we stood strong and were willing to come back for more. We had declared war on him by all means necessary. At that age it was a losing battle. But that was only battles, the war was not over, as a matter of fact it had just begun.

All we had to do was stay alive. From our perspective at that time, it didn't look good for us. But we were soldiers and we were fighting for our mother's honor and her life. The war was on.

About a year and a half later we moved to another house. It was a three-story dwelling. By this time my mother had another child, the first one by him was a girl her name was Shelly and the second one was another boy and his name was Marvin. Now I have another soldier to help in the war. Now she has two of his children and five of us, and another one on the way and her name will be (Anna) when she is born. You would think the beating would slow down because of her pregnancies, but they only got worst. It started to be a normal thing to see my mother with a black eye or eyes, busted lips, swollen jaws, thrown up steps or thrown down steps or just kicked. It just was getting so bad we didn't know from one day to the next who was going to die. It was getting real scary. I have not even talked about the drinking and drugging that was going on between him and his family. We were trapped in a horror movie, which we couldn't escape from.

When the beatings started to spread to my sisters we had to turn up the battle another notch. We stayed up during the night to keep watch on them. He was abusive in every way that people can be abused. Trust me when I said that he was the devil, that's exactly what he was. We would always try to keep a count of everyone because if you were missing, we knew he had someone in a room with the door locked. We heard sounds that were so scary that it was hard for us to talk about. I knew that it was just a matter of time before I was locked in that room with him. I did not know how I was going to react because I didn't know what to expect. Everyone kept what was being done to them to themselves. No one talked about it after they came out of the room with him. Later I found out that he had threatened to kill our mother if anyone told her. So I just kind of tried to stay out of his way, as much as possible.

One day we were playing and it began to rain and we went up to the roof, on the second floor of the house. We decided to go out on the roof and play in the water. Well we were having a great time not realizing that one of us could have fell off the roof and got injured, if not died. Well he came home and found us out on the roof. He went berserk and made all of us come down stairs and stand in a line butt naked. He began to beat us one at a time, for a very long time.

He beat us so bad hat we all had whelps on our bodies as if we were slaves. It was a very bad beating for all of us. One we will never forget. We all had developed a very bad case of bad nerves. When I say bad nerves, I mean bad. Our nerves was so bad that, we could be on the third floor of the house and hear his key just touch the cylinder of the keyhole and we would simultaneously break our necks down those steps, three flights down and run to the living room and sit in front of the TV and fold our hands in a strait line and dear not to make a sound. We would be down those steps before he gets that key in the hole and turns that cylinder. In the beginning he heard us trying to get down those steps and would catch one of us and beat the mess out of us, because all he needed was to hear a sound when he came home and that was enough for him to justify a beating. We had to get our skills together. So we sharpened our skills to the point where no matter where we were in the house we would hear him just touch the cylinder and we would be at that spot in front of the TV without a sound. We were good, we were soldiers, and we were good ones too. Our nerves was shot but we were getting stronger, we were getting more tolerant and we were able to deal with a lot more of the abuse. It was like going through sensitive training in the marines. We were able to sneak up to people or even an animal and they would not know that we were there.

When I think about how good soldiers we were, I think of my next to the oldest sister Jennifer. She is the best. She always looked out for everybody. I remember that Easter, we were getting dress to go to church. The day before, I had broken the toilet in the bathroom. Well that Easter morning my stepfather got up that morning hollering about that toilet. He gathered all of us together in the living room and asked us who broke the toilet. Of curse nobody confessed. So he sent all of us upstairs to our rooms to find out who broke the toilet. And he said that he would beat every one if somebody did not confess. We all went up to our room. Anytime something serious like this came up we would have what you might call court. My oldest brother was the judge; my oldest sister was the prosecutor. And my sister would put some one on the witness stand. Well that day she put my next to the oldest sister on the stand and asked her where were she at a certain time. And she would question her until she caught her in a lie. She was where she said that she was.

Well it was my turn to get on the witness stand, and she asked me where were I and every time I said that I was somewhere they would catch me in a lie. So it came down to that I broke the toilet. I confessed.

So I started crying because I did not want another beating so soon after my last one.

So to my surprise my next to the oldest sister volunteered to say that she broke the toilet. Everybody was shocked, and surprised. We all were also scared. One part of me did not want her to do that. But at the same time I did not want to get beat either. Jennifer went down stairs and told my stepfather that she broke the toilet. She was all dress to go to church. We all were waiting to see what he was going to do. He pulled out his belt and began to beat my sister. He was beating her so long that we all began to cry. He beat her so bad that her clothes were torn to shreds. She got beat worst than anyone of us ever had. He did it because he new that she had taken up for me, and he did not want anyone else to ever think of taking up for me again. My sister standing up for me makes her a real Soldier; she is my hero for life. I will never forget what she did for me and I will get revenge some day.

My mother would let us vent our feeling every time she would go through a beating. She would let us say how we felt, and it was good to be able to vent and get things off our chest. Sometimes she would let us call him names, but not real bad ones. I believe that if it were not for some of those venting sessions, we all would have been bottled up with a whole lot of stuff that we probably would not have known how to handle. I know that it would have been like that for me. I call that unknown therapy. My mother had that kind of hidden wisdom.

Well one day he had gotten very upset about us because we were not calling him dad. I had a big problem with that. Because all I had left to remember my real father was, when he came into town to see us. I remember he took all of us to the park.

I remember that we were at the park in West Philadelphia on Cobbscreek Parkway. I did not find out that it was CobbsCreek Park until later on in my life. I had been riding pass it one day and all these memories of that park came back to me. It had been at lease twenty-five years. I began to cry because it brought back some memories. That were so vivid, they were so real. I remember that I was so happy because all the time that we played in the park with him, I thought he was going to take us back with him when he left. I thought that we were going back home. We were having a picnic and really enjoying ourselves. My mother was happy and we were all back together again. Well after the picnic he put us back into his car and drove us back to our house. When I saw that house I was devastated. I began to cry. I did not want to go back to hell. That's what I called it. I did not want my mother getting beat up anymore. I thought that he came to save us. And get us away from the crazy man. But he was giving us back. I was only about six years old. And I was very disappointed in him. I thought he was our savior.

My mother told me to go into the house as I begged him not to leave. As I went into the house I knew that I would not ever see him again. And I never saw him again. All I could think of was we had a great time together and he went away and never came back. I mourned for him many days before I let him go. Sometimes I still morn for him, even after he passed away. The sad thing about it was I never got a chance to see him again. I never got another hug or kiss. Sometimes I resented him for leaving but most of the time I just remembered the fun we had for the last time at the park. It was not until later in my life that I found out that I never missed anyone as much as I missed him. I always felt that if he had stay with my mother we all would have a different life. I also know that I would not be anything like I am. So I believe that God knew what he was doing. I would not trade me for anything in the world. I love myself, today; I just do not love what I went through.

Well we refuse to call my stepfather our dad. So one day he decided to beat my mother because we would not call him dad. So we had a meeting. We decided to begin to call him dad. It never felt right and we knew that it would not ever fell right. But we did it because it was wartime and at wartime you had to make sacrifices and that was one of them. It was something that we learned throughout our childhood and that there is always a reason to anything.

Mother always told us that common sense would tell you anything, so always use your common sense. Well common sense told us that if we called him dad, mother would not get beat for that. That's one less thing we had to worry about. He always came up with another reason to beat her up.

About two years has gone by now and things were the same. The war was in full gage and we (my brother and I) were on the battlefield every day. One of the girls was missing and we went on an all out search for her. We looked everywhere, throughout the house but we could not find her so we snuck down the hallway on the second floor leading to his room, we heard those sounds in the room and we had to come up with a plan to get him to come out of that room. So we created a diversion outside of his room, we started making all types of noise as if we were fighting. We were so loud the he had to come out to see what was going on. When he came out of that bedroom he went off on us and beat my brother and me for making all that noise. When he came out of that room, my sister ran out of that room holding her clothes in her hand. And now he knew that we knew what was going on. He had threatened to kill us if we told.

He only messed with us like that when my mother was not home. He worked at night and she worked during the day. We knew that we would get beat for disturbing him but it was better that we got beat then arc sister get raped. As I said the war was on and sacrifices had to be made for the better good. We were Soldiers.

CHAPTER 3

The front Line

The sun is shining and I have not heard any disturbances throughout the house today. My mother was at work and for some odd reason all of my sisters and brother was not in the house. They are always up and running early in the morning. For some odd reason I slept late that day. I have been awaked for about a half hour and I didn't know where anybody was. I became a little scared because this was not normal. I sat in my room wondering where the hack was everybody. I was puzzled and confused so I looked out the window at the very sunny day. I pulled the window open and began to smell the air. It was a beautiful day and I was alone and that was a little unusual for me. I just never felt alone like that before.

Then I hear this knock on my door so I am thinking that it's one of my siblings but it wasn't any of them. It was my step dad. He stood at the door and said come with me, and my heart fell to my feet and all my nerves went numb. The bad thing about it was that I was alone. I was all by myself. As I walked down that long hallway all I could think of was, that I was about to die. But somewhere deep down in my heart I said that I will go out fighting because I was a soldier. And a soldier fights to the end. I knew that I was going to lose this one but someone has to die in war so I guess that today it's going to be me.

He led me into his room and told me to take off my clothes. I began to cry and ask him what I did. Please tell me what I did. He said just take them clothes off and get your ass on the bed. I took off my clothes as I begged him to tell me what was my crime what did I do. He became sterner and said, "I will not tell you again. Get your ass on that bed. "At that same time I am thinking and wondering where the belt at, where is his weapon at. All soldiers have a weapon where was his. I was thinking that if he does not have a weapon how he is going to fight. What is he going to use to beat me?

Then it dawned on me that he might be trying to do what ever he does when he takes someone into his room (Making all those different noises, with my sisters.) Now I am really scared because I didn't know what the hack he was doing to them. And I always said that one day it was going to be my turn. On this sunny day he decided, that this would be my turn. So he positioned me on the bed in a weird type of way. I did not understand why he wanted me to get on my knees in the middle of the bed. In my mine I was trying to figure it out. He then was behind me and was positioning himself in back of me and I steal did not understand why. Then I felt this pressure on my butt a pressure that I never felt before. I then felt the pressure pushing on the hole that I defecate from and I had a problem with that. I began to tighten that hole as tight as I could get it. He was determined to penetrate that area and I was not having it.

So I did all that I could think of to do. I lowered my butt as low as I could, to the bed and with my hind legs I swatted like a frog and then I through my butt up in the air with a power thrust and with the force of my thrust I could fell the power in my legs push upward. I felt the weight of his body on my back and I began to lift up and I through him in the air.

For a moment I did not know where he was but I knew that he was not on me. Then I looked up and he was flying across the room. He hit the top of the wall across the room, up side down and the slid down the wall and landed on the floor. For a moment he looked at me and I looked at him. I had a look of surprise and a look of no you will not do that to me look. And he had the look of shock and embarrassment. And for the first time I thought I saw a hidden look of fear. He told me to get my clothes and get the hell out of there. And I did that as fast as I could. As I was going down that hallway, I felt my first felling of victory. I did not know what victory was at that time but it felt great. I had a little smirk on my face but I knew that I might have won that battle but the war was defiantly not over. I knew that he was going to get me in some other ways. You can bet the house on that. But I had that sunny day today. At the age of seven I went up in rank. I felt like a king.

I was right that night he took it out on my mother first. I knew that he was going to do something because he was very angry for the rest of that day. He would not look at me that whole day but I knew that he was going to get someone. That night he beat my mother up and he did it right in front of me. For some reason I got bold and shouted out to him "stop beating my mother "that's all he needed. He grabbed me by throat and hung me up on the wall and was chocking me until I passed out. He then dropped me to floor and I woke up to the screams of my mother. And he saying I will kill that little MF.

I may have had the day but he had the night. As I slept that night I knew he could be beat. And as a soldier I grew up a little and faced a man. At the tinder age of seven I felt we were equal for one moment. I was a seven-year-old man, and a proud soldier on the front line.

CHAPTER 4

The Funeral

The house we lived in at that time was big and a lot of things went on in that house. My youngest sister was born at that time. She was number nine. Yes my mother had nine of us by this time. She was still a young girl at the tender age of twenty-two or three years old. But that woman loved every one of us. She kept us as safe as she could. And we all felt a strung bound together. Because she had to work and leave us home, she made sure that there was someone in charge at all times. She would say when I go to work, James is the boss, if James is not there then, June is the boss, if June is not there then Jennifer's the boss, if Jennifer is not there then Kevin is the boss, if Kevin is not there then Joanne is the boss, if Joanne's not there, then Shelly is the boss, if Shelly is not there, then Marvin is the boss, if Marvin is not there, Anne is the boss. Anne would say whom am I going to boss and my mother would say you better boss yourself. Anne never liked that answer. Until now Terry was born. We all would tell Anne that she has someone to boss now. We all felt so good about terry. It was something about her that made us all just smiles all the time.

She was so precious and pretty. It was just something about her that made us fell so close to each other. She was going on two mouths old at this time. My mother was very serious about that order of authority. She did not play when it came to being left in charge. And we did not play with it ether. When you were left in charge you had a big responsibility. You had to look out for who ever were under you. Their life was in your hands. We all took that very seriously. Someone could have died on your watch. Many times things happened when my mother when to work. The devil was always on the prowl. We all had to take control of a situation, by all means necessary. In this war your age did not matter. You had to grow up and grow up fast, if your turn came up. Rarely did any of the kids under me have to face that responsibility. She dared not put that kind of responsibility on them.

In this house we played everywhere. We were not allowed in the basement, for some reason. I was always curious about the basement. Being a soldier I wanted to know every place that I could use to hide, if I had to. Every time I mention the basement, I was always told that I better not open the basement door. Well I could not take it any longer.

On this particular day I decided that I was going to take it upon myself to find out what was so secret about the basement. So while everyone was out or busy I opened the basement door. A dark cloud came at me. It was so dark that I could not see in front of my face. I did not know what it was; all I knew was that I was breathing these things in. they were mosquitoes. Millions of them came at me as I tried to shut the door but it was too late. I was in shock, I was coughing and gagging and they were biting me.

All I could here was everyone running around trying to kill them and open windows. The whole house was in chaos. They finally got the door shut. But it was too late. The mosquitoes were everywhere. They were biting everyone. We all had to run outside. In the rush someone forgot Terry. When they finally got her she was bitten just as bad as everyone else. It was a terrible day. The police came; they called the health dept. they called the pest control and I do not know who they called, but more and more people was showing up. We were band from that house. The authorities said the band was for forever.

They talked about the sewer was baked up. The waste backed up more than four or five feet high. It was like that, they said for mouths maybe even over a year. The waste just kept building up. With it sitting so long it created a swarm of mosquitoes, which made them multiply and become thicker and thicker.

Anyway the basement became infested with them. The house was quarantined and we had to find another house.

About a week or so later, Terry died. We all were in morning. Everybody was crying, it seamed like we cried everyday. For a long time I did not see anyone not crying. It just seam like everyone was crying forever. We could not stop. I knew that some one was going to die, but I thought it would be one of the older ones. Not Terry. She just got here. Why her why not one of us, why not me. I felt that it was my fault for opening the basement door.

I told my mother that I killed her. My mother said that it was not me that killed her. She said that the mosquito bites had nothing to do with her death. She said she died from something the doctor's called crib death. She said that the doctors do not know what caused her death, but some children just dies for no reason. I did not know what to believe even unto this day.

It was sad throughout the week. The day of the funeral was the saddest I have felt all my life. Everyone was wondering if it was safe for me to go to the funeral. They were concerned that a child my age would not know how to deal with that whole funeral seen. So my mother asked me did I want to go. And I said yes. I did not know what a funeral was. She said that it was the place that you go to say your last good byes to Terry.

I really did not know what death was. All I knew was that some people never was seen anymore. So I was not going to miss the opportunity to say by to Terry, even if it was going to be the last time. Everyone was crying and everyone was sad. When I walked up to the casket she looked like an angle. She looked so beautiful. I stopped crying when I saw her. The funeral was really nice and I will never ever forget her. We all miss Terry even up to today.

CHAPTER 5

Hezekiah the King

For reasons unknown to me, we had to move again. We move to 26th and Harlem Street. It was a small, one way street with a big wall at the end of the street. On the other side of the wall was the police station. It was a small house it was not as big as the one we just left. So we all had to sleep together. It was different but was not like we were, all bunched up before. The fighting and the abuse continued. Mother was still getting beat up and we were still getting beat all the time.

One night he beat my mother up and my oldest brother could not take it any longer, so he ran up to the bedroom and jumped on his back and began to pull and beat on him to get him off my mother. He turned around and grabbed my brother and began to beat on him like he was a grown man then he took his head and began to bust his head against the wall. He did it so long that my brother's head bust open with blood. He would not stop slamming his head against the wall. We all shouted and cried and begged him to stop. My mother began to beg him. He stopped and said that the next time one of us jump on him he was going to kill her and us too. We picked my brother up and took him to the bedroom. His head was bleeding badly. My stepfather would not let my mother take him to the hospital.

So she went to the store and got some gauze, bandages, hydrogen peroxide and ointment. She fixed him up pretty well. We all helped change the bandages when my mother was at work. She would always say that we were going to get away from him one day. We believed her and we just could not wait.

Christmas came that year and we did not get anything. We woke up on Christmas and no one was home, just us kids. We did not know where my mother or stepfather was. The whole day went by and we did not have anything to eat. We would cry but that did not make any difference. It began to get dark and still nobody came home. So we just sat around. The electric was off and there were no heat in the house. Now it was completely dark in the house and still no one came home.

Then about ten o'clock at night, some one knocked at the door. We were afraid to go to the door because it was against the rules. We knew that we were not supposed to answer the door for no one. So my brother went to the door and peeked through the curtain. He said its grandmother. She said open that door. So he opened it for her. She said for all us to come over to her house and eat. She said "It doesn't make no sense they have not fed you kids all day". "Come on over my house now."

So we put on are coats and walked over to her house. She lived across the street. She fixed us a big dinner. We were so happy and full that we did not know how to act. That Christmas turned out to be ok. I remember that it was one of those very cold wintry nights; it was snowing like a blizzard. I do not know when my mother and stepfather came home that night. I just remember being woke up by some loud hollering. My mother was saying to my brother to help her get him back in the house, before the police came. I got up and went to the front door and saw my stepfather walking down the street without any clothes on. He was naked and talking to himself. My mother and brother were out in the blizzard trying to get him back in the house. I found out that he was drunk and wandered outside in the snow. The snow was blowing so strong that you could not see in front of you. When I looked down the street all I saw was his body shape. He was too drunk to fight. They got him in the house just in time. People were coming out because he was making a lot of noise. That was a winter and a half.

The weather changed now and it was becoming a very good summer. I use to go to the store on the corner when I had a penny or two. The storeowner's name was Mr. Ben. He was a good man and for some odd reason he took a liking to me. One day I came into the store and I had three cents. And I wanted some cookies. While I was looking in the counter trying to chose what kind of cookies I wanted. I saw some of the cookies were broken. So I asked Mr. Ben how much it was for the broken ones. He began to laugh. He almost fell out of his seat.

He said what you mean. I said if the whole ones are a penny a piece than how much was the broken ones. He just laughed and said since you asked me that I don't know. Nobody ever asked me that before. He said you could have two broken cookies for a penny. I was happy because there was not that much broken off of any of them. So it seamed like I was getting two for a penny. After that when I came into the store I would only buy broken cookies. And he would laugh every time. He began to call me Hezekiah. From that day on my name was Hezekiah. I did not find out until I was grown who Hezekiah was. He was a good king in the Bible. That is when I knew that I was royalty in my spirit.

Mr. Ben found out that it was my birthday that summer and came outside of his store door, the morning of my birthday and said "Hezekiah Hezekiah come here" so I came down to his store and he said come in I have something for you. With a smile on my face I said what is it. He gave me a box. It looked like a shoebox. I thought it was a pair of shoes. When I opened the box I was devastated I could not believe it. It was a whole box of broken cookies. I said all these cookies for me. He said yes I saved all my broken cookies for you. They are all for you, now go on and play. I will see you later. I said thank you and went back down the street. When I got down the street all the kids were out playing and we all sat on my steps and I shared my cookies with all my friends. Everyone treated me like a king. Especially the girls, they all wanted to be my girlfriends.

It really got crazy that summer. They began rioting on 22nd street. I believe President John F. Kennedy was assassinated. Any way they were rioting that night. And my stepfather was at work so my mother heard that they were looting and people were running down the street with all types of stuff on their backs. They were grabbing TV's, stereos and all types of things. My mother told us to stay in the house because they were shooting. My mother decided that she was going down there to get her something. We cried and begged her not to go but she went anyway. About an hour later they were carrying her back with blood running down her leg. We thought she was going to die. She had a big peace of glass in her ankle. It was sticking out of her ankle and everyone was scared to take her to the hospital. So she just pulled the glass out and blood began to gush out of her ankle like a geezer. They put a towel on it and tide bandages on it to stop the bleeding. They bandaged her ankle up and she could not walk for almost a mouth. We used to tease her and say that at lease she did get some nice hand towels and a blanket.

My step father beat her for that too. He was mad at her because he did not want, to go around the rec. center to get the surplus food. Nobody wanted to go get the food. The only ones that were not embarrassed about going to get the government food were my mother and I. We would get the shopping cart and fill it up with the cheese, butter, caned beef, caned peanut butter, powder eggs, powder milk and some other stuff. We did not have a problem getting that surplus food. Nobody wanted to go get the food but they did not have a problem eating it. He still made her get the government food. We went proudly too.

I always went to Mr. Ben's store and brought those cookies until we moved off that block. He always made sure that he had some broken cookies to sale to me too. I know that it was a few times that he broke some on purpose just to make sure he had some. He was sorry to know that we were moving off the block. So the day that we moved he gave me a box of cookies to go. I never saw Mr. Ben again. I always remembered him calling me Hezekiah. He recognized me as being a king at that early age. I did not know it then, but I know it now.

CHAPTER 6

Finding My Way

So many things happened after we found another place to live. We move to 22nd street and Columbia Avenue. (Now call Cecil B. Moore Avenue.) We had a lot of fun as children on this block. My grand mother (his mother Martha) was a very nice woman. She was short and chubby, but she was a strong woman. She was the perfect grand mother. She had a strong belief that cleanliness was close to godliness.

She got us up every morning by 7:00am. While the girls were in the bathroom getting wash, the boys were outside scrubbing down the front steps. We had to scrub those steps down with bleach and pneumonia, but when we got finish with those steps they were clean. They had those white marble type steps back then. After the girls were finish washing up, then it was our turn to get washed. When we all were finished she would have all of our clothes lined up and ironed out. She would get us all dressed; fed, and then she would line us up on the steps outside. It felt so good to be clean. People would walk by and say look at those children they are so cute and clean. Some would say, are they Rose's kids.

I have to hand it to my Grandmother she did that everyday. It gave me a feeling of self-pride. I still have that felling today. Now during the day, when the liquor started getting pulled out and we started getting dirty outside, her attitude would change. The drunker she got the dirtier we got. By the end of the day we all were call every name in the book. Her favorite word was "Dirt Devils". When my Grandmother got drunk she was not always nice to us. She would beat us and call us names. At times she would hug me too much and the smell of that liquor would make me sick. Some times she made us sleep in her bed. I did not like doing that at all. When she got into the bed with me, that liquor smell would almost smother me every time. They would sit around all day drinking. That was a normal day. A day with out liquor was like a day without the sun. You know the sun came out everyday and so did the liquor. Other than the drinking she was a great woman. When it came to punishment she would tell, who ever it was, to go out back and get her a switch. Sometimes I thought she love to beat us. But I changed my mind when she would say. "You guys know what your mother goes through, why you are making me whip you. And you know what your father will do." She would some times be crying. But she did not shed one tear when she was drunk.

The neighborhood that we lived in was basically bad. Gang warring was a big thing at that time. The civil rights movement was going on at that time too. The biggest thing happening then was the music. The music in the sixties was real big. My mother and step dad was always hanging out. All of us kids always listened to the radio. We always had on WDAS "Goergie Woods the guy with the goods". He was the biggest DJ in Philadelphia. He would sponsor Christmas parties at the recreation Center on 22nd and Columbia Avenue.

We were members of the rec. center during the day. Every year they would have a Christmas party for all the disadvantage children. That is basically how we got Christmas presents, in those days. If it was not for the Christmas party I don't think we would have gotten any presents. One day we went to the daycare center to get on the bus, to take us on a field trip. My sisters went with my brother and me. They jumped on the first bus and I being a hard head jumped on the second bus. It turned out that the two buses went two different directions. We thought that we were going to meet up at the same place but we didn't. My bus took me to the Strawberry Mansion area. And they went to the park, to have a picnic. I got off the bus and followed everyone into the building and every one went his or her own way, and left me standing there. I was only seven years old. And nobody cared where I belonged.

So I decided to go back outside. I looked across the street and saw a park with swings and things. So I went to the light and waited to the light turned green and crossed over by myself. I was proud of myself. It was about nine in the morning, the sun was shinning and it was summertime. What more could a boy ask for. I had the whole park to myself. So I play and played and played all by myself. It started to get hot and I did not have anything to eat or drink. I remembered that my sister had my lunch bag. I sat under a tree for a while and then I went back to playing. That helped me forget how hungry I was. Hours went by so I decided to go back over to the place where they dropped me off and see if I could find someone to help me or at lease get me home. When I got there no one was there everyone had left. So I went back to the park.

Now it was getting late I new that it was almost late afternoon and I began to get scared. I was not going to ask any one anything because I did not trust grown-ups or strangers; something in my spirit told me not to let anyone know that I was alone. So I went and sat on the bench hungry and scared wondering what was I going to do. Then it came to me. I remembered that when that bus left the rec. center it went strait and the only time it turned was when it came to that house and parked. So I put two and two together and said that I was going to walk strait down that street. My mother always said that common sense would tell you anything. I just thought I was using common sense.

If I walk straight I might run into something familiar. I came from 22nd and Columbia ave. and I was at 33rd and Columbia Avenue. At that time I did not know it. So I began my journey down Columbia Avenue. From 33rd. it was amazing what I saw. It was summertime and every body was out. I saw all types of people. I passed the record shop where they were playing music I stopped and listened to the music. People was dancing some were just hanging around. I kept walking. I walked passed restaurants, the food smelled so swell but I kept walking. The more I walked, it seemed like the more I saw. People were doing all types of things. I felt like a grown up, like I was on my own. Nobody questioned me or asked me why was I by myself, or anything like that. I just kept walking. Then it happened I started to see stores that I remembered, places that my mother took me to. Then I knew where

I was. I started to walk around the corner from my house and as I was turning the corner I herd a shout "There he is". It was my oldest sister. She was so glad to see me and then all my family was running up to me asking me where I came from and where was I. They were so happy to see me and I was happy to see them. I told them all about my day. My grandmother told every body to give me some air. She said look at that boy he has not eaten all day. They treated me like a hero. They said that boy found his own way home at seven years old, after being lost all day. That was good, they all were so proud of me. My mother just cried, that's all she could do. It was a great day and a great adventure.

CHAPTER 7

The Move Out Of the Ghetto

We had to move again. This time it was for the better, that's what they were saying. But I have to admit that the house was pretty nice. It was a two-story row house, in Southwest Philadelphia; the Street we moved on was, 1314 South Ruby Street. In those days around 1964 the area was predominantly white. In two years my whole block turned predominantly black. I think that it was, only, about two white families left.

The move was nice we all helped move the furniture and stuff. It had three bedrooms. The boys stayed in one and the girls had another one. And of course my mother and Step dad had the main one. All I could think of was, where the exits or hiding places were,. Something in my spirit made me fell good and something made me fell bad. My mother had to work to help keep the house so I new that we had to go through some changes with this new move. My mother said that he got a good job with the city. And she will be around more. But I knew that my mother was trying to get away from him and she was going to work as much as she could. Just like I thought the fights were on again. We were not in that house one good day and the fights were on.

I had to get back into my combat mold. My older brother never jumped on him again after that beating he got at the last house. But he was not a quitter. We stayed on guard all the time. My step dad became an alcoholic and did his worst damage when he was drunk.

Whatever job, he had, he would return home almost everyday drunk. I believe that when he got drunk he would remember me throwing him across the room. Because he always came home and found me doing something he did not like and he would beat me. Sometimes I don't even be doing anything. I was so tired of being beat that I use to become immune to them. Sometimes I don't even think I felt them. But he seams to find some kind of belt, switch, stick, rope, extension cord or something to get me to cry.

We all went to elementary school I was in the third grade. School was like a refuge; it was the place to go. It was the only way of getting away from him. We all loved to go to school. Some time he would keep my sister home for whatever reason. And I would get sick and he would tell me to get my but out of the house and go to school. I could see in my sister's eyes that she did not want me to go. So I stayed outside until school got out and I would come into the house making all types of noise. But he would have already done his dirt. And she would be sad and we would set there for a while and not say a word. And then she would change her attitude and get back to her happy go lucky ways. I know she was still hurting inside but we played it off like we did so many times before.

Another way that we got away was going to church. One time my mother got beat very badly and the preacher from around the corner herd about it and came to our house, to see if he could speak to my stepfather and my mother. My stepfather did not want to talk to him. The Pastor invited my mother to come to the church and bring us. His name was Pastor Peterson. After that we were in church every Sunday. Pastor Peterson was a white man and it was my first involvement with white people. He was one of the nicest people I have ever met. He looked out for us. He would come if we had to get some help for my mother.

During that time of the civil rights movement, all you would hear of was what the white man was doing to black people in the south. With all the lynching and killings, I thought that all white people was bad and wanted to beat black people. So when I saw white people I automatically felt some kind of way. Sometimes when we went to the store on Chester Avenue the white people would call us niggers and we would call them hunkies. We live on 54th and Chester Avenue and everyone from 55th street and up was white people.

All the blacks were below 54th street. I never knew what a hunkie was. I just called them that because every body else called them that. After meeting Pastor Peterson I made sure that I did not say anything like that around him. I really tried to stop saying those words all together. But you know how peer pressure is when you are around your friends. When we went to school we had to go into the white neighborhoods. And everyday we had to fight our way home. They had a gang called the Dirty Addies. They were a tuff group of white kids and grown ups. If they cult you, you got beat up. When we got out of school they would get out an hour early. And they would be waiting for us. We had to run home everyday. But when they were going to school we did not have to be in school until a half hour after them. That's when we would get them back. They used to go to school all beat up and we would get beat up after school. Most of the time it was fun, except when one of us got beat real badly. I think they were having fun too.

One day it was about ten of us and they had an event at the recreation center on 58th and Chester Avenue. We all went to the event. We all were having a good time when the Dirty Addies showed up. They were at lease thirty of them. They surrounded us and it was nowhere to go and we were in the middle of a big field. After they surrounded us they began to close in. we stayed together and they had sticks, bats, chains, and we did not have anything. The fight was on and we tried to fight as much as we could then we heard everyone saying run. It looked like a fight at the ok Carrel. We all ran and when we got back to our neighborhood. We all sat around and laughed for a long time. The good thing was no body got heart.

Anyway back to the church. Pastor Peterson was a great pastor. I do not remember his preaching much. We were at bible class and church every Sunday. One time he let us do a talent show. So we all put together our acts. Well the day of the show our parents came and the pastor was there with his wife. They all sat there and when the show began, you could tell they were a little uncomfortable. We had done the Motown review. My group sang a song from the temptations (How I wish that it would rain). I was the lead singer and I thought that I was the next Smoky Robinson. After the show was over the pastor said that, he was hoping that the show was a little more biblical. We all laughed. He allowed us to enjoy ourselves.

We could not wait for Easter. It was the only time we got new clothes. My mother would dress us up and we would be cleaner than the board of health. For me it just felt so good to be in a suit. I felt important. Easter was the only time for me when I could forget the craziness that was going on in my house. It was when I was in church that I felt his comfort. The way the pastor talked about Jesus I knew that he was going to show through sometime. And he was going to save me from the devil that we lived with.

CHAPTER 8

Cookies

Some times when I went to school, my friends and I would go into the super market and buy a loaf of bread, and while someone was buying the bread the rest of us would steal the rest of the ingredients to make sandwiches. I would go to the deli and order a pound of baloney and a pound of cheese. And I would stuff the meat into my pants and sometimes I would be the one who would buy the bread too. Anyway we would walk out the door and we never got caught. We would get out of the store and run around the corner and make sandwiches. And have a great time. Well we talked about it to everyone because we thought it was funny. So we told everyone how we were getting over on the super market. This went on for about two or three weeks. We were having fun we never got caught and we was eating lunch everyday.

Well I came home from school one day and my oldest sister came up to me and said you better stop stealing those cookies. I told her that I was not stealing cookies. I told her that I never stole any cookies from anywhere at anytime. She said that's not what the word is, going around. I said that I did not care what people are saying; I did not steal any cookies. Well everybody was talking about it and I began to get worried. Because everybody was saying things and I did not want it to get back to my mother, and especially my stepfather. The word got to my mother and she came to me and said were you stealing cookies and I told her no. She did not believe me, for whatever reason I do not know. She decides to grab me by my collar and drag me out the door, down the street, around the corner, all the way to the supermarket. The supermarket was three blocks away. She dragged me pass all my friends and if anyone was in her way they moved when they saw her. She was not playing and they new it. She throws me into the supermarket doors. She asked the cashier "Where is your manager, I want to see him right now". The manager came up to my mother and said may I help you. She said yes, my son stole some cookies from this store and I want to pay for them right now. He said we did not catch him in here stealing. She said, "I know he stole some cookies and I want to pay for them." How much are your cookies. He said what kind you are talking about. She said "I don't give a fuck what kind they are black, white, peanut-fucking butter;" "just tell me, how much your cookies are." He said that they were two dollars and something. She paid him and told me to apologize to him. As she was slapping me up side my head. I apologized to him for something I did not do. At lease it was not cookies.

Then she apologized to him for me and pushed me out the door, and dragged me back down the street. Back to our street and back into the house. She told me to go upstairs to my room and don't look for any dinner. So here I am on punishment for some cookies, cookies. I went to bed without any dinner that night; I got up the next day and went to school. Some of the kids on the block talked about it but for the most, part nobody said anything. My sisters and bothers did not say much either. They knew that it was only the beginning of a punishment. We did not know what was going to happen when my step dad found out. Oh he just would have a ball with something like that.

I returned home after school the next day and when I walked into the house he was lying on the couch. He had his back towards me. So I was walking by him to go up the steps. He turned around and said what have I been hearing about you stealing some cookies. I said I was not stealing any cookies. Just like my mother he did not believe me. He jumped up off the couch and grabbed me and through me down on the floor. He began to kick me, and then he took off his belt and began to beat me with it. The belt broke so he grabbed the cord that goes with the TV. He beat me with that for about fifteen minutes. That flew out of his hand, so he began to punch me like a man. He told me to get up stairs and take off all my clothes.

I went up stairs and went into my room, took off my clothes and sat on the bed. He took a long time so I lay down. Then the door flew open and he came at me real fast, he ran over to me grabbed me by the neck and at the same time he threw the window all the way up, and with out a moment's notice he threw me out of the second floor window. I was dead I knew it as I was flying out the window and all I could think of was, this, was the day that I was going to die and meet my sister Terry. Just as quick as he let me go he grabbed me by the ankles and pulled me back into the window. I was shocked I did not think that he could catch me in time. I was trying to get my thoughts together then he through me against the wall. He came over to me and grabbed me by the throat and lifted me up on the wall at the same time he was choking and shouting, "If I ever hear that you were stealing some cookies, I will kill you. Do you hear me" all the time I was trying to say yes, but how can you, when you cant breath with his hands around your throat. He choked me so long that I pass out. All I remember was waking up on the floor butt naked. He must have continued to beat me because I had welts all over my body. Blood was coming out of them. I just lay there thinking that I would never steal again, especially cookies.

I am a soldier and all I knew, was, that he was still trying to win the war. Well, the only thing he won was another battle. The war is not over yet. I made up in my mind that one day I was going to win this war and the only way, was, he had to die. The war is on now. The real hard part most of the time was recovering from the beatings. Your wounds took so long to heal. The sores and the scabs sometimes became infected. It seems like as soon as I recovered from one beating I was getting another one. I knew what my mother was going through. She got beat more than all of us.

I believe that if it was not for the family meetings that we had. We would not have survived a lot of that insanity. When we had our meetings my mother would allow us to vent all our feelings. We were allowed to get our feeling out and say what was on our minds. Sometimes she let us call him names. We had a meeting after every beating. I know that it helped me a lot. Because if I was not able to speak my mind, I think I would have kept it all bottle up inside of me. Until one day I would have exploded. My mother would always say one day we will not have to go through this. One day.

CHAPTER 9

The birthday

My birthday was coming up and I was going to be eight years old. I was getting older and wanted to run away from home, like my brother. There was a time when I hardly ever seen my brother any more. He would not come home much. After school he always had something to do. So it was basically up to me to keep an eye on my sisters. I was the soldier on duty. I did my best to keep the devil from ravishing my sisters. He still was getting drunk almost every day. And he still was beating on my mother. She was getting stronger, some times she stud up to him. We decided to tell my mother what was going on when she was not home. He always threatened us about telling her. He would say that he would kill her and my sisters if anyone of us ever said anything. I was getting to the age that I did not care any more. We wanted to say something but my sister told us not to say anything yet. So we did what she wanted. I protested but I respected her wishes.

My birthday was the next day and I was feeling ok. That night they were fighting, because he was accusing my mother about cheating on him.

He began to punch on her and I ran into the living room and he looked at me and said that I better get the fuck out of there or he was going to kill me. I told him that I was not going anywhere and I said beat me instead of her. Before anything else was said my mother told me to go up stairs. For some odd reason he left out. He must have had something to do or he went and got drunk.

The next day I awoke to a beautiful summer day, July 9, 1965. I was eight years old. Everyone said happy birthday to me and that made me very happy. My mother gave me five dollars. It was the first time I had a whole five-dollar bill. I thought that was great. It was something about this birthday that was different from all the others. I just could not put my finger on it. Everything seemed different for some reason. People looked at me different they just did not act the same that day. My friends seem to treat me nicer. As the day went on I just went with the flow.

It was about six o' clock that evening. I was setting on my steps by myself. And I looked down the street and I saw my stepfather coming up the street. I started to get up and go into the house. Something told me to stay right there. So I stayed. He walked up to the steps and stood there for a minute. As I watched him I noticed that he was not drunk. He had on nice clothes, and he had a smile on his face.

This was not normal for me. I was used to seeing him coming up the street with a look of anger or drunk or staggering. Not this day. He was different. He said to me "Today is your birthday." I said "yes". He said come with me, I am going to take you out to dinner. At that time my mother and some of the kids came out of the house. And they were amazed at what they were hearing. My little sister said "Dad's taking Kevin out to dinner" and all the other kids in the family were so surprised. He had not taken any of us out ever. This was the first time that he ever did something like this. He has not even taken his own kids out on there birthdays. I knew that it was some thing about this day. History was being made. We walked up on the avenue; there was a real nice restaurant on 56th and Chester ave. It was sort of high class. The area was still prominally white at that time. We walked in and the hosted seated us. I sat down and he sat down across from me. All the time we walked to the restaurant we talked like a real father and son. It was as if we never had any confrontations before at all. I could not believe the conversation that we were having. I just could not believe it. For a moment, I thought that I could love him. Just for a moment. I had to snap myself back to reality. It was too good to be true. He told me to order anything that I wanted. I said anything and he said anything. So I ordered a stake and potato dinner.

It reminds me of when my mother and I would sneak off, and she would take me to a restaurant and we would set there and eat and talk for hours. While we were waiting for our food we talked about everything. He sounds like a fine guy. He was decent. I started to see what it was that attracted my mother to him. He had a certain charm a certain way about him that made you forget about all the things he did. But in the back of my mind I had to remember that he was the enemy. And the enemy was not to be trusted. All through dinner we talked. After dinner he asked me did I want desert. He said go ahead this is your day. Have some dessert. So I did. I began to eat my dessert and it was good. I had chocolate and vanilla ice cream. He sat up strait and stretched his arms. Then his whole demeanor changed. All that charm disappeared. He looked at me as if I smacked his mother. He said I wanted this to be your day and wanted you to enjoy this outing. Tomorrow I will be back on your ass. You act like you wanted to stand up to me. Well I am letting you know that I will fuck you up. I know that you don't like me and I don't like you so starting tomorrow we will be back to normal. He had a look of hate on his face and I put on my soldier face. We looked each other strait in the eye. Eye to eye we were on the same page. He said we are going to tangle again and you will lose. And I said no I will not.

He said, "There is one thing I want to say to you". I respect you because you are a real warrior, you are a fighter and I respect that. And I said I respect you to. We shuck hands at the table and he paid the bill and left a tip. As we were walking home he said "If you jump in the middle of a fight with me and your mother again I will kill you." I did not say anything because I knew that I would jump in the middle. My mother asked me how was dinner and I said that it was ok. I never told any one about that night. I knew that it was between him and me. I knew that we were going to meet up again. I felt like a man the way he talked to me, as if he was dealing with another man. It gave me a feeling of maturity that was new to me. I went to bed that night and felt stronger then I have ever felt.

My brother used to beat me up until I cried. He used to say I am beating you this way because no one will be able to hurt you. They will not hit you as hard as I am. I never respected his philosophy until I got into fights with boys my age. Their punches did not hurt just like my brother said. I remember one time the guy next door to us, little brother, who was just one year younger than I was. He began to hit my sister. I told him to stop or would bus him up side his head. He said he would bust me back if I did. I told him just don't hit her again. I began to go down the street and he hit her again. So I bust him up side him head.

I punched him hard in his head. He began to cry and he ran and got his older brother. When he came up to me he asked why I hit him. I told him that I asked him not to hit my sister and he did it anyway. He proceeded to tell me that I better not hit him again. And I told him that if your little brother is big enough to hit my sister he is big enough to get hit. So he said if you hit him again I will hit you. And I said and I will hit you. So he said we can fight right now. And I said lets do it than. We began to fight. He punched me a few times and I did not fell the hits. They did not heart, so I stood my ground and did not back up. He through a punch to my head and I blocked it and punched him in his eye. He then grabbed me and we fell to the ground. I got on top of him and began to punch him in the face. All of a sudden my brother was pulling me off of him. And his mother was stopping the fight. After the fight I sat on my steps with my sisters and they asked me "do your back heart "I said no why? They said that when I had that boy on the ground, his little brother was punching me in the back. With all the excitement I did not fell him hitting me in the back. But when I went to bed and woke up the next morning. My back was very sore. One thing I know is that I was able to take their punches but they were not able to take mine. My brother was a brawler nobody wanted to fight him. They said when he fault someone he went crazy on them. I knew that when he was hitting me he was doing it out of love.

CHAPTER 10

The Street

The street that we lived on was a fighting street. It seamed like everyone was fighting. The people of the block were always fighting. They were always starting fights with each other. If the woman was not fighting, it was the men; if they were not fighting then it were the kids on the block. Sometimes everybody was fighting. Like one time some new people moved on the block. They were bragging to everyone on the street that they came from Germantown. Which is another part of Philadelphia? Anyway they were saying things like they were better than any one. My brother was outside one day talking to some of his friends when one of the guys that lived in that house began to tell my brother and his friends that they were making to much noise outside of their house. My brother told them that they lived in a free country and they could talk as loud as they wanted to. But he also said that they would go down the street. But these people in that house just moved on the block and act like they had been living on the block for years. The guys in the house began to say that my brother and his friends better get away from in front of their house.

They did not know my brother and really did not know how crazy he could get. They just kept on taking saying stuff like they could get their boys from G-Town to come up here and turn this street out. Well that was the straw that broke the camel's back. One thing they did not know was that my brother was from a gang too. He was from Woodland Ave., one of the biggest gangs in West Philadelphia. My brother walked to the corner and said out loud Ho Ho. And with in about thirty seconds hundreds of guys were coming around the corner. I mean hundreds of guys. The block was so full of people there was no standing room. I was on our porch looking at amazement. The people that were, doing all the talking ran in the house. The guys ran up to my brother and asked him what was going on and he said, the people in that house was giving him some problems and that they said that they were going to bring some guys down from G-Town. So they said what you want us to do. He said lets f—them up. They began to through everything that they could find to though into the peoples house. They were thronging rocks, cans, bottles, and trash cans. When I saw them through a big trashcan through the front window I did not know what to do. I became afraid for those people.

After they bust all the windows out, they went up to the door and kicked it open and they ran in the house and pulled the guys out and the house and began to beat those guys up. I did not believe that they went right by their mother and their father and grabbed them out of that house. The people called the police but that summer the police was so tired of breaking up fights on our block that they did not even come that night.

After they beat those guys up, just as quickly as that gang came they left even quicker. In seconds they were gone as if they were never there. We all sat on the porch and just laughed at what had just happened. The peoples house was so messed up I could not recognize it. They went into those people's house, they through all of their furniture out on the street. They ransacked those people's house. I felt sorry for them. The next day they had a truck moving their stuff out. We did not see or here of them again.

One day my mother was walking down the street with my grandmother and some women was saying that my mother thought that she was cute or something so my mother did not pay them any attention. So they just call her names. On their way back from the store the same women stated saying something again. My mother just ignored them and kept walking. Two of them decided to come off the porch and get into my mother's face. My mother did not want to fight these women but they wanted to fight her. So they got in her face and started to call her bitches and whore.

My grandmother told her to just keep on walking and do not pay them any mind. Well they were not taking that. They wanted to fight. Just as the women started to push my mother we all heard a loud shot someone had a gun and they were shooting. Everyone started to run. All you could see was people running up the stairs. When they thought that it was going to be a fight everyone was in the street but when they heard them shots they all went a running. I looked up and saw my stepfather shooting; he was shooting in the air. As he was shooting he was saying you people want to fuck with my wife come on I will kill all of you mother fuckers. Come on back, where are you motherfuckers now. My mother and grandmother were running to. They ran into the house. My uncle (my stepfather's brother) grabbed the gun from my stepfather and he jumped into his car and road around the corner. And my stepfather went into the house.

The police came around the block just as he went into the house. All of the people were saying he got a gun. So the police ran up to my door and said come out or we are coming in. So my stepfather came out and said what is going on. The police said where are the gun and my father said I do not have a gun. They searched him and they looked through the house and did not find a gun. So they decided to leave. The people started saying his brother got it. The police did not search him or the car. The police new they would not find the gun. So they left. Those women did not say another word to my mother after that.

When everything was over my stepfather's brother came back in the house, with the gun. He gave it to my stepfather and they laughed about it and in that moment while they were laughing they did not know that I was watching every move they made until it happened. I saw where he hid the gun. That's all I needed to know. Now I had access to another weapon. I am a soldier and I need to up grade my arsenal. In this war you never know when you just might need it. In my mind I was thinking that it might come in handy.

CHAPTER 11

The Truth Comes To Light

My oldest sister began to get sick a lot. She was throwing up and she just was not looking well at all. She would say that she was all right but she would get sick again. My mother decided to take her to the hospital. When my mother got back home that day, she had a look on her face that I have never seen before. She never looked like that before. She had this look like she wanted to kill somebody. That look was familiar. I remember having that look. I remember my brother had that look. So I knew what that look, looked like and I knew what it meant. The only thing I did not know was why. Why was she that mad? Why did she want to kill someone? I knew she did not want to kill my sister because she was holding her to close. I knew that we did not do anything. Something in my spirit said the devil did something again? Every time I saw that look it always was because he had done something. Now I was real mad, all I wanted was to know what he did. I needed to know.

I asked my mother she would not say anything at that time. Nobody was talking for a couple of days. And then my mother called a meeting. We all sat around waiting to find out what was this meeting all about. My mother asked us "did your step father ever touch any of you in your private areas"? We all were scared to answer her because we did not want her to die or get beat up. She said tell my right now and nobody will hurt you. But I need to know right now. So the truth comes to light. We all started to tell our stories. The more we talked the more she cried. She said for us not to worry about her crying, just tell me everything. While we told of our experiences she just held all of us close to her and cried like a baby. Once we started to tell her we could not stop. I was hearing stories that I did not even know. Then she told us the big news. We did not know the real magnitude of what it meant at that time, but it did not sound right. She said that my oldest sister was pregnant. We were wondering who was her boy friend because we new she did not have one that we knew of. We knew how you got pregnant but did not know whom was she dating. It came to us. Then all of us had that look on our faces. We just wanted to kill him. And we did not have a problem showing it either. My mother told us to not do any thing crazy. She said that she was going to take him to jail. And it had to be done right. And she did not want us to say a word.

My mother approached him about it and he denied everything. He swore up and down that it was not he. He even wants to fight about it but the way my mother stood up to him, for the first time, he backed down. I know he backed down because he knew that he was wrong and the last thing he needed to do was get bad. My mother told him that she was going to get him locked up. I know that scared the mess out of him. He had gotten locked up before and got into that jail acting like he was some big man or something. Those guys beat him up so bad they put him in the hospital. So I know that he did not want to go back there. So he kind of backed off her for a moment, and just kept denying it. My mother filed the papers at the child abuse center in the Frankford section of the city. We went to that center almost everyday giving interviews. It seamed like each one of us had to go on a different day. We almost lived up at that place. They interviewed all of us and asked all these questions. Sometimes they would bring us back to ask us the same question over again. We were so tired of going up there and back, that it just became a pain in the butt. My mother almost lost her job because we had to be there almost all the time. We miss so much school too. Sometimes we would say mother do we have to go through all of this. Is it worth it? She would always say yes it is so stop complaining. We would do as she said. After all that we went through. Then we had to wait.

My mother knew that with a case like this he would go to jail and we would be free of him forever. That was her motivation. We knew that he would be gone forever too. So now we played the waiting game. He would come home and for the first time he did not make a big stink. He kind of mined his business and we minded ours. My mother did not talk to him and we did not say anything either. This went on for about two mouths. My mother would call almost everyday to find out the results. They always said that it was still under investigation. We just did not understand that if my sister is pregnant how much more do you need, she is only eleven years old. What do you need to investigate? Just lock him up. That's all they need to do. Why were they dragging their feet? We just did not know why.

Finally they sent my mother a letter in the mail. It stated that they did not have enough sufficient information to file charges on my stepfather. She just cried and cried and cried. Then we cried and we got real mad we just did not know what to do. My mother went down there and raised hell with those people. They just stuck with their story. Then my mother found out that he new some people down town at city hall. And they got him off. Somebody did him a favor so that he did not go to jail. I am still looking for that guy.

After he got off with that he went back to his old ways. He began to get drunk and came home starting fights. My mother was getting to the point where she did not take his abuse. She would say some things to him that I knew would get him mad. I would tell my mother to please do not agitate him. He still was crazy.

CHAPTER 12

The Confrontation

My mother's attitude began to change. After my stepfather got off with those abuse charges, my mother did not have any respect for him at all. She did not care what he did or what he said. She just changed. She was always careful about what ever she did because my stepfather was very jealous. She knew that if she got caught cheating he would kill her or beat her to deaf. She should have left him years ago. Now she seems to be making all the moves that she should to make it happen.

Some guy came home from the Vietnam War and his mother lived across the street from us. He and my mother began giving each other the eye. I knew that it was going to lead to some confrontation between my mother and my stepfather. I knew that it was going to happen if they continued to relate with each other. The word was starting to get around. I knew that the other women on the block were going to make sure he would get the word. One of these days he was going to find out. I just tried to look out for her. At the same time protect her from getting her butt beat up. My oldest brother was always gone. I knew that it was up to me to look out for her.

One night my stepfather went to work and as soon a he left, my mother asked me to come over Miss Jean's house to get her if he came back home, during the night. Miss jean was the mother of the marine from the Vietnam War. His name was Timmy. I pleaded with my mother to not go over that man's house but she went anyway. She told me that every thing was going to be all right. Just keep an eye out. I knew that she was wrong and that it could get her in trouble. My nerves were already bad, and she was not helping them any. I was so scarred for her. But in a way, I felt that if my stepfather did confront him, than I would see a marine and an army man get it on. We are all soldiers so let's get it on. The best man wins my mother. I just hoped that if my stepfather won, he did not kill my mother. Then I would have had to kill him. She put this record on (Stand in my corner, by the delfonics) and said to keep the record playing until she came home. I stayed up all night listening to that record. It played over and over again. All night long I listened for the door to open. This was pretty hard for a nine-year-old boy. All I could think of was my stepfather coming home and finding her not there. I know that he would have gone off. And beat the mess out of her. Every hour I would look at the clock and wish she would get home before he got there.

My heart was in my shoes for every second that went by. Finally she came home it was about six in the morning. I asked her what took so long. She would say do not worry, I will be all right. About seven o' clock that morning he came home. He did not act like he knew anything. So I went to sleep and boy did I need it? That day went by and I felt that she got away with it. I told her that he was going to find out. The people on our street love, to see fights. They always try to keep something going. She said that she knew what I was saying but she was going to do what she wanted to do. She said she was the mother and I was the child. In the back of my mind I was saying but you are acting like one. If she knew what I was thinking, she would have popped me upside my head. That night my stepfather came home from somewhere. He was drunk as a fish. I was upstairs with my sisters. We heard them arguing and then the fighting started. His brother had come home with him. When I heard them fighting I ran down the steps and at the same time that I was coming down the steps. He punched her with a punch that I have never seen. I have seen him punch her many times but this one was different. He her hit so hard that she spend in a circle and fell out on the couch, when she hit the couch her hand flopped over like she had died. I never saw her fall like that. I stood on the steps for a second to see if she would move but she did not. I hollered her name but she did not respond. All I could think of was that he had finally killed her.

So I ran up the steps thinking that since he killed her I was going to kill him. I remembered where hid his gun. I went right to it. I got the gun and started down the hall to go kill him. I heard him down there cussing and calling her all kinds of names. (Mother fuckers, bitches, and a whore). I went down the hallway and my oldest sister stopped me in the hall and was begging me to not go down the steps with that gun. She was afraid that he would take it from me and kill me with it. She just did not understand that I was a soldier and it was wartime. I had the upper hand I had the gun. At the same time that she was pleading with me she had sent my other sister to get some help. Well she came back with my stepfather's brother. He came down the hall towards me and I told him to stop. I pointed the gun at him and told him if came any closer I would shoot him. He stopped. He said Kevin please don't go down there and kill him please. I told him to get out of my way. He said Kevin in a tone that made me listen. It was a kind of tone that was like pleading and at the same time begging with tears in his eyes. I had tears in my eyes too but I was crying because I thought my mother was dead. He said Kevin your mother is not dead. He said Kevin if you give me that gun I promise you that you will never go through this again. He said, "I promise he will never beat you, your mother or your sisters again." He pleaded with me to believe him.

I am standing in this narrow hallway making the decision of my life. My sisters are all crying and pleading with him. All I can think of was I am a warrior. I am a soldier and a soldier does not ever give up his weapon. I cannot give up my weapon. If I give up my weapon then I will be venerable. And he will kill me. Then in my spirit I looked into his eyes and I saw sincerity. I felt that he was going to do the right thing. The little time that I spent in church I, new that there is a God. So for whatever reason I put my faith in God. My spirits said give him the gun.

With tears poring down my face and his, I handed him the gun. He took the gun opened it and turned towards the steps and said come with me I will stop this. I followed him down the steps with my sisters right behind me. In that house when you went down the steps you would come to a landing and there are three more steps to go into the living room. While following my uncle down the steps I ended on the landing he went the rest of the way down the steps. My stepfather was coming out of the dinning room at the same time. My mother was still on the couch in the same position. She did not move.

When I reached the landing my uncle walked towards my stepfather with the gun extended it out to him, saying look at what your son was going to do to you. My eyes widened like they never have before been. I was shocked that he gave the gun to him. He gave my weapon to the enemy. I was so shocked I did not know what to do. I looked at my sisters with a look like I am going to die. And why did they stop me. I was mad at my self because I gave my weapon away. I gave it to the enemy. Now I am going to die. While I was thinking I was looking at him give the gun away. My stepfather looked at me and said you little motherfucker while he was pointing the gun at me. He said I am going to kill your little ass. He began to chase me up the stairs. I turned and ran up the stair. All the time I am thinking where can I run, can I get out on the roof? I was trying to figure out some means of escape. I did not have a plan for this; I did not think I needed one. I ran up the stairs and as I got to the top of the stairs looked behind me to see how close he was. I was praying all the time. As I looked back I was wondering why he all of a sudden stopped chasing me and turned around and began to run back down the stairs.

I heard him say no bitch you better not go anywhere. My mother at that time started to run out the front door. He wanted her to stay in the house more than he wanted me. He tried to catch her but she got out the door and began to run down the street. He ran out the door and began to chase her. We ran down the step and out the door, watching her run and him chasing her. We began to holler to her run mother run. He kept on running after her.

He tried to run through some water and slipped and fell on his but. We all was in the doorway and began to laugh at him and he turned around and looked at us laughing. He got up and started to come back to the house saying I am going to kill you mother fuckers. We were just kids and were not thinking we forgot that our mother just ran off and we were home alone without any protection. And he was coming back. We stopped laughing and ran in the house, and tried to lock the door. We knew that he would break the door down, because he did it before. I tried to lock it anyway. When he got on the porch we heard him taking to someone. So I went to the door. To listen to whom he was talking to. It was the marine from across the street. So I opened the door and stood there to hear what was going on. The marine telling my stepfather that he needs to stop beating on my mother and us.

My stepfather said that he should mind his own business. He said that he knew that they were missing around and that he was going to fuck them up. The marine said that he did not know what he was talking about. And stop beating us up like that. My stepfather said shut the fuck up and mind your business. Out of nowhere the marine punched my stepfather right in the jaw. My stepfather fell on the porch and began to get up. All of the people on the street were out and watching what was going on. All my friends were looking. Everyone was looking for this big confrontation. I wanted to see this more then anyone. I needed to see my stepfather fight a man.

He beat my mother, he beat my brothers, he beat my sisters and he beat me. I needed to see him beat another man. I really thought that he was a bad dude. Just as he was getting up off the porch, my mother was pulling up in front of the house with the police. They were jumping out of the wagon. My stepfather put his hand on his jaw and said in the most girls' voice that I have ever heard. He said to the police "did you see that, he hit me" he sounded like a girl. I was shocked. Where I come from if someone hit you, you hit him or her back. This man embarrassed me because as a boy the last thing you want to see is your father act like a bitch. He was not my real father but the rule still applies. He acted like a bitch in front of all my friends. How can I go to school with that image?

At that time the marine stated that he was a police officer and showing his badge he said that my stepfather was drunk and for them to lock him up. The police hand cuffed my stepfather and started to pull him away. As they pulled him he started to shout I will be back and I am going to kill all of you mother fuckers. And I shouted to him come on back if you want to but this time I will kill you. He shouted and when they though him in the wagon I told him tomorrow I would kill you, so come on back if you want to. My mother told me to shut up and don't say anything. After what I just been through I was not going to take nothing from anyone. I was a man I was a soldier. We all went in the house and was on pins and needles all night.

I was ok because I knew that I was not afraid any more. I knew that when he got home he was not going to go through this house like he did before. He left acting like a bitch and that is how he was going to get treated. It was a long night.

CHAPTER 13

The Decision

I stayed up all night. I waited all night for him to come through that door. Every time he got locked up for beating my mother. The police will always take him to jail when they were called. They would always let him out every time at six' o clock in the morning. He will always come walking through that door at six-thirty in the morning. Well it was six-thirty and just like clockwork he came walking through the door. I had my knife in my hand. My mother told me to please go up stairs. I went up to the top of the stairs and sat down. I waited while they talked. They were in the dinning room and I could not hear what they were saying. All of my sisters and my brother were behind me at the top of the step. We all were waiting to see if they were going to fight again.

They spoke quietly for about an hour. My mother came upstairs and told us to come into her room. My stepfather left out of the house. I made sure where he was because I was the look out. So we all go into my mother's room to have a meeting. So we asked my mother what was going. She said be quiet and let me talk. We were all as quiet as mice.

She began to tell us that he said that he was sorry for a lot of things he did and all that stuff. We were like mother we herd that before. She said be quiet and let me finish. She said we are going to get a divorce. Some of us did not know what that meant but the ones that did go along with the celebration. We all jumped in the air about ten feet high. We jumped for joy and started to dance around the room. My mother started shouting very loud she said be quiet there is a condition. In an instant we stopped and said I knew it I knew I knew it. What are his conditions, does he want the house? Does he want us to leave the house? What does he want? My mother started crying with her hands in her hands. We all stopped talking and asked her what was it he wanted. She was quiet for a moment and said he wants to take his children with him, when he leaves. They were the three youngest. They began to cry and say they did not want to go with him they wanted to stay with us. And we said we do not want him to take our brother and sisters. We said he couldn't have them. My mother said I do not want to give my children away. So we all said no. Then my mother said if he stays, then it's going to be some hell up in here.

She said that she refuse to take any of his stuff again. At that time I began to think that it might be better if he leaves verses him staying. I had enough of his abuse and

I know that we all felt the same way. So we called a meeting with just the kids. We all sat around and voiced our opinions and we convinced the three youngest ones that they might be better off with him. We told them that he had the good job; the money and they did not have to share it with all of us. We told them that he always spoiled them anyway. And they had to admit that he did not beat them like he beat us.

So they were getting the best part of the deal. All we were trying to do was get rid of him so that we could get out of this nightmare. My stepfather knew what he was doing. He was trying to tear us apart. He was trying to tare my mother down. My mother refused to separate her children. And he knew that. His mother came to my mother and said. If you let him have the children I promise to look after them. And whenever you want to see them just call me and we will make some arrangements. My mother cried like a baby the day that he left with them. We all cried and hugged and kissed each other and told each other that we will always stay in touch.

Before my stepfather left with my sisters and my brother, he pull my mother to the side and said "if you ever try to contact my children or try to see them at any time I will kill you." That's why my mother was crying as hard as she was. They all got into his brother's car and drove off. I had a feeling of joy and sadness at the same time. But I knew that we were going to stay in touch with each other and I was going to see them again. But I was so glad that the devil was driving out of my life. It was then that I knew that there was a GOD because he answered my prayers. I always had a lot of respect for his brother. I truly believe he had a lot to do with him deciding to leave. Until today I believe his brother told him that we were getting bigger and one day we were going to kill him if he kept on beating on our mother. Between my brother and me he was going to die. He made the best decision in his life as far as I am concerned.

A good month had not gone by since we were living in that house with my mother when she called a family meeting. We all came together to hear what was going on now. We only had meetings when something big was going on. That whole month was a good month because for the first time I did not have to be a soldier. I thought that I could just be a kid.

This meeting stopped all of that. I found myself getting back on guard. Being responsible. My mother began the meeting with. I love you all very much. And I want you to know that I will never do anything to hurt you and I will be there for you all, know matter what. We were a little confused because we did not know what she was trying to say. She finally said I am moving out. But I can't take you all with me. We said where are you going? She said that Terry and I are going to get an apartment.

We said where are we going to live? She said you all are going to stay here. We said with out you? She said yes.

We said we do not want to be here by ourselves. She said that we would be ok. Jim and June will be the boss of you. Just do what they say. We said they are not our mother. She said what I said. Just do what they say. She said I would not be far away. And I will be back every week and make sure that every thing is all right. I will bring you all some food and money. But I have to go and I will be back. As usual we would get into our group and ask each other question. My sister said look at it this way we will be our own bosses we do not have to worry about somebody telling us what to do. We will be on our own. We all laughed and said you are right. Let her go wherever she wants to go. We will be on our own. We will be grown. By the end of that week she was gone. We were left home alone. We had to look out for ourselves. I was nine years old. I thought that my mother was not going to stay away long, it lasted two years. She did come through every two or three weeks to see us and give us food and money or what ever she had.

That's when I began to learn a lot of responsibilities. I was faced with a lot of issued. My first issue was when I went to school. The first few weeks I got up and went to school sometimes I did not wash; sometimes I just pulled some clothes out of a pile and put them on.

Until one day I noticed that all the kids seemed to all be laughing at something and I did not know what it or whom it was. Until a boy who I guess did not care about how I might have felt. Said you stink and you dress like a bum. And everybody began to laugh at me, and pointing his or her fingers at me. They said that I did not have a mother and I was a poor child. I was devastated I did not know what being totally embarrassed felt like until then. That day when I got out of school I ran home and did not want to go back again. I did not want to face them ever again. I cried and told my sister what had happened. She said you got to go to school. She said I would tell mother that you need some new clothes. She said but in the mean time you got to wash your own clothes out and iron them. I did not know how to do that. She said I would show you how to wash your clothes. After my clothes were dry she showed me how to iron them. My brother came home that day and said what are you doing? I said I am ironing my clothes for school. He said that's not how you do that, you are supposed to iron pants like that. He showed me how to get a real crease in them. When he got finished with those pants they looked like they came from the cleaners. Then he showed me how to iron my shirt. When I was finished it looked like I had brand new clothes. I hung them up and shined my shoes. He showed me how to shine my shoes too.

When I was finished I look at those clothes all night long to make sure any one did not touch them. I all most stayed up the whole night because I could not wait to show off my new look. Those kids were not going to laugh at me again.

I got up that morning and took a nice bath and made sure that there was not a dirt speck on me. My face was clean and when I put on those clothes I looked like a brand new hundred dollar bill. I looked like money. I went to school that day and when those kids saw me there was not one thing that they could say badly about me. They just said stuff like look at him he is clean as the board of health. I felt good that day. I learned that being talked about was not good for me unless they were saying something nice. From that day on I never went to school or anywhere without looking haft way decent.

The responsibility that my mother left on me was bigger than I could handle at that time. But just like the other stuff I went through I took it. I am a soldier and sometime we got to fight. This was one of those fights. I was determined to keep up with my personal hygiene. I learned to care about myself and I liked doing it. That's one thing that my grandmother did leave with me was cleanliness is Godliness.

CHAPTER 14

Now the Fun Begins

Now that we were on our own we did what ever we wanted to do. It was a whole new and different experience. It just seemed to be so extremely different. We could do what ever we wanted. When other kids got called in the house, we could stay outside. We could stay up as late as we wanted. Nobody could make us do anything. My oldest sister was my only boss, and of course my oldest brother. They were my friends. They let me do what ever I wanted to do. It was always something going on in our house. Everybody wanted to do what he or she wanted to do. Sometimes my oldest sister would just do stuff to get us up set. She had all the control. She had all the money. She controlled the food. And she used those things to her advantage. They would send us to the store all the time. One night we all were very thirsty, so my sister and brother sent my next to the oldest sister and me to the vending machines that were outside of this store on Chester Ave. about two thirty or three o'clock in the morning. We had about five sodas in our hands. We began to walk home when I saw a police car following us. So I began to run and holler at my sister to run because the police were chasing us. I ran down the street and jumped into some bushes and lay down so that the police would not see me. My sister kept on running and the police stopped her. The police came right to the bushes and told me to get out of the bushes or they would send in the dogs. I jumped out of those bushes. They took us to the 35th precinct.

On 65th and woodland ave. they asked us all type of questions'. They put us in the police car and took us home. The police asked my sister where our mother was and she told him that she worked the night shift. The police released us to my oldest sister. You have to understand we all were children. Children are going to do childish things. And that's what she did. In a regular household with a mother and father, they would brake up fights or stop one child from being unfair to another one. In our case there was no one to stop the injustice or the wrong doings. My sister was the queen and whatever the queen wanted the queen got even if it meant that you got hurt. That was the same with my oldest brother too. What he said goes or you got beat.

My oldest brother and oldest sister knotted heads a couple of times too. My brother would win. But my sister did not back down. They would come to a compromise. My oldest sister was a prankster. She did stuff to you just to see the look on your face. She would have someone throw a cold glass of water on you while you were sleep. That's one of the worst things some one could do to me. She would do that and I would jump up and no one would be around. And then I would here them laughing in another room. I did not think it was funny. I would be so mad but who could I call, who could I tell and how could I make her stop? It was not always peaches and cream. My sister was like that, and she had all the control. You had to be careful not to sleep around her sometimes. One time she put a match between my toes and lit it and they all ran. I woke up and my toes on fire. It was always a joke going on in our house. The name of the game was to not be the joke. You always wanted to be the one playing the joke. We did all kinds of things to each other. My sister had control over the money. She would buy candy and give it out according to her needs. She would have us go get her a glass of water. She would say that the one that gets her the coldest glass of water would get some candy. We would be running water from upstairs and down stairs and bring her some water. She would test all the glasses and say they were not cold enough and send us back.

All she wanted to do was see us running up and down the steps trying to please her. Then she would say one of us won. I was always her favorite and my sisters would complain but it was what it was. My oldest sister knew that I always looked out for her. We were close we were very close. She let me do anything I wanted to do. Over all she was fair most of the time she just like to laugh. She just had to pull a prank on one of us every now and then. She got some of the kids on the block too. We would stay up all night. We would have company some times too. The parent on the street would not let some of their kids come over because they new that we were home alone. We never did anything real bad we just did what we wanted to do. The other kids were a little jealous and always told their parents some of the things we did. No matter what we did we all got up and went to school everyday. We did not miss school. School was important to us. We knew that we were good kids and we did not get bad grades. We always wanted our mother to be proud of us. She would always give us extra money around report card period. We wanted good grades anyway. One reason was we did not want to get my mother in trouble. If the school knew that we were home alone they may have tried to put my mother in jail or something. We never gave them a reason to investigate us. We were never absent from school or late.

On the weekends my sister would make a big breakfast. She would cook bacon, eggs, sausage, pancakes, home fries and toast, every Saturday. One day she said I don't feel like cooking, one of you has to do it if you want to eat. So I went in the kitchen and I cooked that day. I saw her do it so many times I felt that I could do that too. I burned myself so many times you would not believe. It was not the best breakfast but every body eats it. It was good for my first time. After that I started cooking on the weekends. I got better and better. After a while we all started to cook on the week ends. Then we started competitions. We wanted to see who cooked the best breakfast. My sister was real good. But she left some dishes when she finished. I did not leave any dishes when I finished cooking. Because I learn to clean as I cooked. I was the best cook. All my food would be hot and the only thing left to be finished was to clean the plate you eat on. I was good. I started to get good at cleaning my clothes, ironing, cooking and sewing. I became very domestic. I felt so grown; the only thing I did not know how to do was make money.

One day I was playing with my friends. We were running up and down the alley. When one of my friends said lets go into the Marley's house. They went away. The Marley's were the last white people left on our block. They were a good old couple. They mind their business and stayed to their self. We went in the back window. And someone opened the back door. Well we had ourselves a field day in their house. We found all types of things. I found a gun. It was real small. We found some old coins and a little bit of money. We sat down at their kitchen table and eat their food. We just were having a good time. We were so dumb we were all in the front window laughing and the neighbors saw us and called the cops. Someone hollered at us and said we called the cops you all better get out of those people's house.

We ran out of that house and down the alleyway. Everybody went his or her own way. I ran to my house. My sister was on the porch watching the whole thing. My sister said you did not get enough of stealing. And when she said that, she brought me back to those cookies. And I said I forgot and you do not have to remind me no more. I never stole from anyone since that time. That beating I got from my stepfather was enough for me to never want to steal again. I guess he did have some positive impact on me after all. Just the memory of that beating scares me today. I decided to get my money from somewhere else. I knew that however I got some it would be honest.

Being home alone had a profound affect on all of us. We were subjected to a lot of things, such as sex.

My oldest sister would bring her friends over. And they would talk about sex and stuff. I did not know what everything it was. But her girlfriends would say that I was there little boy friend. They would kiss me and touch me and rub me. I did not know how to deal with it at first. Then one day I asked my older brother how do you kiss? He put his lips a certain way. And stuck out his tong and started to wiggle it at me and say that two people are suppose to put their mouths together and play with their tongs. I thought it was the nastiest thing two people could do. My brother always seemed to know what he was taking about. Even though it was nasty I could not wait to try it on one of my sister's girlfriends.

One day my sister's girlfriend came over. And I came down stairs and she said there goes my little boyfriend. She said come over here and gives me a kiss. As I walked over to her I was nervous, because what I was about to do was nasty and I did not want her to smack something or me. She put her arms around me and pulled me close to her and put her lips on my lips and at the same time I took my tongue and pushed it into her mouth. I was very careful not to push it in her mouth to hard. I did it nice and slow. As my tong went into her mouth, her mouth opened and her tong met my tong and for almost a whole minute we let our tongues slowly move and mingle together.

When we kissed before it was just a peck here or a peck there. But this time, she acts like she did not want to stop. We were so involved in our kissing that she forgot all about my sister. My sister had to shout at her and tell her to stop. This girl did not want to stop. Then she came to her senses and said where you learned to kiss like that. I just smiled. She kept me next to her the whole time that she visited my sister. Every time she got a chance to kiss me she did. She let me touch her anytime I wanted to. I would touch her breast and her butt and her between her thighs. What ever I want to do to her that day it was all right. I loved every moment of it. I did not know that it felt so good to touch a girl. From that day on she would come over to see me even when my sister was not home. She just loved to kiss me. She must have told some of her friends because my sister was having a lot of company. All of her girlfriends wanted me to be their little boy friend. Everybody wanted to feel how it felt to kiss me. I kissed them all. Some of the older guys that they hung with were jealous of me. I was only a kid. My sister told her girlfriends that if they wanted to kiss me they had to let me touch them anywhere I wanted to. And they did. I was in heaven at that time in my life. Nine years old.

My sister had girls over all the time. They talked about sex all the time.

One time my sister made this girl lay down on the floor. She told her to let me do it to her. I did not know what to do. My sister said pull down your pants and get on top of her. I was embarrassed but I was also excited too. I got between her legs and put my thing in her and my sister would say push it in and out. As I was doing it, I felt this strange feeling in my private area. It felt like I had to pee or go to the bathroom. But I kept on pushing it in and out. Then I got scared because she was acting like I was hurting her and she sounded like she wanted to cry. I began to stop and my sisters said don't stop keep on doing it. So I kept on pushing into her. It got to the point where I could not take it any more. But I did not want to disappoint my sister so I kept going. The girl began to shiver and scream and I could not hold it any longer. Something began to come out of me and I began to get scared because I thought I went to the bathroom in her. I got up real fast and ran to the bathroom. I wanted to finish peeing in the toilet. When I got upstairs to the bathroom I did not have to pee. I looked at my private and it had some white stuff coming out of it. I got really scared then. I thought I broke something. I went and told my sister and she said don't worry it was nothing. She called it (come). I did not even ask here what she was talking about. That girl never let me do that to her again but some of her other girlfriends did. It got to be a normal thing that kids did at that time.

My sister would let me go with them to the all night drive-thru movies. I thought that it was so much fun. Everybody was having sex and fooling around. I thought that I was grown-up like them. Come to find out, they were not that much older than I was. We were at an age and time when the sexual revolution was at its all time high. People were doing their thing. Having sex in the sixties was the thing to do. The music was all about love and peace. We were in the mist of three revolutions, the sexual, music and civil rights revolutions. At my age I was getting hit with all three of them at the same time.

I honestly believe that, the struggles that I go through today, as far as being a womanizer and a very sexual person, comes directly from my early years. The only thing that keeps me grounded at this day and time is my determination to being the best Christian that I can be. Like I said I am a solder and now I am fighting a different fight.

My sister was about to have her baby any day. So we were all trying to get things ready for her. That is one of the reasons her girlfriends were over all the time. It was going to be just a matter of time before she had to go into the hospital. I woke up about three in the morning my mother was taking my sister to the hospital. I knew that this was the time.

We all waited all morning to here what she had. Then my mother came to the house about ten o clocks that morning. She told us that she was ok and she had a boy. We were all happy. We could not wait to see her and the baby. I am an uncle. I did not know what all I was supposed to do but it sound good.

CHAPTER 15

The Newborn King

It was September 24th 1967 a very beautiful day. We all were sitting on the steps when we herd my youngest sister say, "Here they come". We all jumped off the step and ran down the street to see the newborn king. We all gathered around my sister as if she was a celebrity. Everybody wanted to see him. We were so happy to see him. We were all uncles and aunts. At our age that was a big deal. We did not know what the responsibility level of being an aunt or uncle was, but we wanted to be one anyway.

We followed her into the house where everyone got a chance to hold him. We loved him from the beginning. He was so precious and cute. He was so tiny with big bright eyes. We knew he was going to be all that, because we were going to take care of him. We all took care of him. We spoiled him. We gave him anything he wanted. We would even have fights over him. Who would get the chance to change him or just hold him? It got to the point that we had to put everyone on a timer or some kind of schedule.

My sister still went to school every day. The lady across the street took care of him in the daytime.

She was only twelve going on thirteen. We all went to school everyday and all of us would break our necks getting home to see who was going to get him first. It was always some kind of commotion going on at that time. We nick named him "Doo Doo Bug". It was a funny name. We did not know much but we all taught him everything we knew. My brother and I became role models and we wanted to be good ones. So a lot of the things that we did wrong we made sure that we did not do it in front of him. All of us were very cautious about what he saw.

As I said before, we were coming up at time in life when all type of things was going on. We often asked each other when or how we were going to tell him how he was conceived. That was something we did not want to tell him at all because we were not at all happy about how he got here. We really wanted to put that behind us and never talk about it again. But we knew that somebody was going to tell him. We just wanted him to here it the right way or at lease from one of us.

Now it was six of us living in the house alone, without any mother or father. We were very happy at that time. We had a responsibility now. We wanted him to be a good person and we worked hard at keeping an eye on him. People began to talk. They wondered how we could live in the house and raise a baby at our age. We showed them we did not have a lot of people coming and going in and out of our house. We did all the things grown-ups did. We were responsible.

We all had a quality of some sort. My oldest brother was the authority figure. He was the first king and we all respected him of that. He would make sure everyone was ok no matter what it was. We could always count on him. Even up to this day he steal holds that position. My oldest sister June was the prankster and his mother. She could come up with some kind of prank at any given time. She was also the mother figure. The mother in a way where she was the authority we also respected her in that kind of way. Jennifer was the caretaker she showed everybody how to take care of our selves. Jennifer took care of all of us. She looked out for us all the time. James learned the art of sacrifice from her. At one time or another Jennifer sacrificed herself for all of us. James began to act like that.

I was the storyteller. I told him a story about everything I wanted him to learn. I put it into a story form. He went crazy about my stories.

There was always some kind of morrow or wisdom to my stories. He would always ask me to tell him another one and another one until I ran out of stories or got tired. He learned a lot from my stories, the good and the bad. My stories was so good that his teachers told him that who ever is telling him these stories must began to read from a book. The slang that I was using was not proper English. So I stopped telling him stories like that.

Joanne was the debater. She had to debate about everything. She was so controversial. She wanted to argue about everything. We called her the philosopher. She seemed to have a philosophy about everything. Sometimes she was right and somctime she was not on point. At that time she had a bad habit of lying so we did not know when she was telling the truth. We had to break her out of that. We did not want James to grow up lying about things. We told her that if she kept on lying we were not ever going to believe her again. And we meant it. She believed that we would not ever believe in her so she began to tell the truth. She did get better. From what we have been through it was very important that we believed in each other, because we were all, that, we had.

Now Shelly, Marvin and Anna were separated from us and they were cut off from seeing James. They did not get to see him until he was maybe ten or eleven year's old maybe earlier than that. They were in some way half brothers and sisters. Something we never wanted to talk about or bring up. They began to have a relationship from than on and we all were reunited from that point on. We began to get together as frequent as we could.

We all went through some trying times as the years went on but we made sure that James was always looked after.

James was the fourth king and he turned out to be one of the most outstanding one of us all. He was a solder and he made sure that the events that caused him to get here was not going continue to through his children.

James was about twelve or thirteen years old when I received a call from my oldest brother telling me that james was locked up for molesting a seven or eight year old little girl in our family. We found out that he had been released to his mother until his trail came up. He had heard rumors about his real father, but he really did not get the real story.

My brother and I sat him down and began to tell him about our pass. We told him everything from the beginning to the end. We told him about what we had to fight against from the time we first came to Philadelphia. What kind of man his real father was. We told him about the beatings his grandmother suffered through. What his mother went through and what we all had to endure. We did not say these things in a way that made him fell like he was going to be like his father. We told him that all we were telling him is that the buck would stop with us. The ways of his father will not be tolerated or accepted in our family. If he wanted to remain a part of this family he had to make a decision on what kind of man he was going to be.

We all began to cry. We cried in each other arms. He said that he was not like that and he was sorry for what he did. He said that he would never do anything like that again. He could not stop crying and nether could we. We held each other for about fifteen or twenty minutes before we began to hug each other. It was at that moment that we all created a bond that could never be broken from that day forward.

The court system was not so easy on him. They decided that James had to go to a boarding school until he graduated from high school. They said that if he finishes high school they would expunge his record. That is exactly what he did he graduated from that school with the highest GPA and with honors. We went to his graduation and we had not been more proud of any one as much as we were for him. We all supported him throughout his years in the school and when he came home he was a man. He was one of the most decent man that I have ever met or had the honor to know. I respected him to the at most. Personally he was a better man than I was. I was still dealing with some things that I did not recover from at that time. He was way passed me. I began to look up to him in a lot of ways. He never stopped looking up to my brother and me. He always looked at us as if we were his fathers.

All we were was a couple of kings above him, mentoring the best we could. We just held our positions. We were solders looking out for each other. We knew that we would always be there for each other no matter what. We loved each other with all our hearts. He grew up to be a great man, father, nephew and KING. He will always be remembered for his honor, loyalty, Love and his high level of a sense of humor.

CHAPTER 16

The Surprise Move

I was outside playing with some of my friends, when I saw my mother ride up in a car with Terry. They got out and went into the house. I left my friends and went into the house to see them. I did not see my mother that often so I wanted to see how she was doing. I also wanted to get some money. But this time it was different. They were smiling and all happy. They sat us down and called a family meeting. I really wanted to hear this it seemed strange for them to come like this. They never called a family meeting since they left us two years ago. I was wondering why they are calling one now.

We all were shouting, "What is it". So they told us. "We have gotten married and we brought a house" we all looked at them in a very surprising way. We were shocked. They said "we came to get you all so that we can be a family at our new house again." We didn't know what to say, we were in shock. It all sound good, the house that we were living in was in bad shape anyway. We all thought that it would be great to live in a new house all together. They told us to get into the car so that we could go see the new house.

So we all jumped into the car and road over to the new house. The house was on 52nd and Addison Street in West Philadelphia. We all jumped out of the car and ran up to the house. It was the first house on the block close to 52nd street. The house was across the street from the park (Black Oak Park now known as Malcolm X Park). It was a nice neighborhood and the house was a whole lot better than the house on Ruby Street. We ran all through the house and everything about it was nice. We laughed and shouted that we had a new home and we were going to move in it and be the perfect family. We believe that we can be the family that we always wanted to be.

I was eleven years old and we were on are own for two years. For some reason I felt that something was not right. I just could not put my hand on it. We were all excited and happy to be able to say that we were leaving the old house. So much had gone on there. We had so many memories at that house. All the events that took place there was so over whelming. We told all of our friends that we were moving and some were happy for us and some were sad. I just had a couple of friends that I told but we knew that we would see each other at school.

My only problem was that I had to start catching a bus to get to school. That was going to be different for me. The other thing was I was moving to a different neighborhood and I did not take into consideration that I was moving to another gang location. Where I was living the biggest gang was "Woodland Avenue". I was moving to "Cedar Avenue's" area. Now that was a challenge. I was often mistaken for one or the other depending where I was. I did not let it bother me too much, because I was not from either one of them.

I was eleven going on twelve and graduating out of six grades. I was going to Jr. High School and we were moving to our new house. All of these things were going on at the same time. I just took thing as they came. I did not know that my life was about to be turned upside down. Things were never going to be the same. I will just start with the move to our new house and our new family arrangements. The first month was ok we brought our normal ways to our new house. We felt that we could act like we were home. Well the quote unquote grown ups in the house thought that we were acting like children. We lived on our own for two years and we did not have a problem, why all of a sodden there is a problem with how we act. I just did not understand it. So we called a family meeting. We were told that we were trifling, dirty children, who needed to grown up and act like we appreciate what people do for us. We asked them to explain what they were talking about.

They said that we did not keep the house, our rooms, and ourselves clean. And they said, "We think that we can do anything that we wanted to do at any time that we want to do it ". Well they called the meeting to inform us that we were no longer going to do what we wanted to do. They said that for now on we had to follow all of there new rules and or we were going to get beat for it. Well that did not stand well with us. We were not going to be told what to do by some grown-ups; we were just as grown as they were. We were not going to have it. They gave us a list of demands. 1. Get up five in the morning and clean all of the woodwork and baseboards throughout the house. 2. Clean up the kitchen. Also clean up the dinning room, front room, bedrooms, hall and steps. 3. Wash ourselves. 4. Fix breakfast, 5. Get dressed. 6. Get out and go to school. This should be done everyday. They called it K-P duty. As if we were in the service. We have shifted from one extreme to another.

It started to come to me why we were doing all these duties. Terry had not too long been home from the Vietnam War. He was a marine in the war. So I began to put two and two together. He missed being a drill sargant or something and some how felt that he could change us. He wanted to use some military tactics on us. He did not know that I was a soldier at five years old. I know what it is to be in battle.

Fighting for some thing I believe in. going through war with someone who was trying to kill me. I knew what it was like having bad nerves. I knew what it was like being beaten closed to close to death. I knew what it was like losing battles. He just did not know whom he was dealing with. He threatened to beat me. I laughed at that statement. I have been through more beatings than he has. He does not know what it's really like to be beat. He can only imagine. I found myself back at war but this time with a different enemy. This one was bigger and he had a profound look on his face. He looked like he was determined to change us. As time went on he did not beat the girls he just beat me. He always had this smirk on his face when it came down to beating me. I began to take it personally. My sister and I stayed on punishment. We were determined to do what we wanted to do. And no one was going to change that.

They began to call us rebels because we stayed in trouble. Every time you looked up we were on some kind of punishment. For over a year he and I fought. He was a Philadelphia police officer and I was a twelve-year-old boy. I still stood my ground, as much as I could.

One time I stabbed him with a knife. We told him that we were not going to let another man hit our mother. He knew what went on at the old house. So this one day he was drinking and got upset with my mother about us and began to argue.

He tells her to shut up and she say no, she will not shut up. He hits her so I told him he better keep his hands off her. He tells me to go sit down and stay out of it. I told him no and he better not hit her again. He says if you don't go sit down I will hit you. I told I was not going anywhere. He smacked me in the face so I smacked him back. He begins to chase me. I ran to the kitchen and pulled out a knife and as he ran towards me I stabbed him in the arm. I could see the moraine come out now and he was about to attack and all I could hear was "mothers cut mothers bleeding" I immediately opened my hand and let the knife drop to the floor. Some how in the mist of the fight she got between us and the knife cut her on the arm? It was not a bad cut it was a flesh wound. The fight was over but I knew that the war was not. My mother began to cry and say that she did not want to go through all the fighting again. We told her we did not want to see the fighting come back ether. With the drinking that my stepfather was doing I knew that he would do it again. And sure enough we herd some noise up in their room one night. But this time my older brother was home. Just so happened he came home to visit that night. We heard them arguing. We were all listening to hear if the arguing was going to get louder. Then the next thing we knew my mother holler for my brother. My brother told me to get the knife. I shot to my room to get this bayonet that he gave me from the service.

By the time I got the knife he had already brooked the bedroom door down. And when I got to the bedroom he was on the bed grabbing him by the neck.

My mother was screaming for him to stop and I was getting ready to stab him. My mother screamed so loud you had to listen to her. She said "he did not hit me he did not hit me". We did not want to hear it.

We told him not to put his hands on her period. My mother said stop so we did. That's the only thing that saved his life that day. My Mother said she did not know that my brother was home. She said she was just calling him because Terry looked like he was going to hit her. She said she would not have called him if she knew he had come back at home. We all calmed down and we told terry that we are not playing when it comes to our mother being beat on again by any man. From the look on his face he believed us that night.

CHAPTER 17

The Party

I met a friend in school. I was in Jr. High school now, twelve going on thirteen. The friend I met his name was Slick. We were in science class one day and the teacher was talking about the ameba (a single cell animal). The way he explained it was so funny that it made the whole class break out in laughter. He called the ameba Al he explained how Al the ameba broke himself in half and started dating sue ameba. Ha Ha. You had to be there to understand it. Anyway the friend I met was very interesting guy. He was a year older than I was. He came from a family of eleven brothers and sisters. He was on the bottom half. His father made him hustle after school to bring food home. So every day he would go out and shine shoes. I found that to be fascinating. So every day after school I would go out with him and help him shine shoes. We became good friends.

We went from 52nd and Woodland to 52nd and Market Street to all the bars. I did not know that we could make that kind of money.

On a good weekend we could make two or three hundred dollars. I began to learn the business and made my own shoebox. Slick was good at spit shines and when he put a spit shine on a pair of shoes they shined.

Well one night we both went to a bar on 52nd and Market Street and I decided to give this guy a spit shine. So I spit on this man shoe and he went crazy. He took his free foot and put on my chest and pushed me to the floor. He shouted, "You little mother fucker you spit on my shoes. I should kick your ass." Before I could say that I was sorry, about five men jumped up and beat the shit out him and they through him out of the bar. They took some of his money and gave it to us. They did not let anything happen to us in the bars. I did not believe how much respect they had for us. I believe they respected the fact that we were hustlers, working for an honest dollar.

I began to hang with Slick all the time and we became inseparable. We went everywhere together. We started to experiment with drugs. We smoked pot and began to drink. Some days when we would go over to his house his father would say "where the food at". He would send us back out to make some money to buy something to eat for dinner. He would say and bring back a fifth of liquor. And we would make enough money to buy food and liquor. We would bring the food and liquor back and while his sister cooked the chicken we would help his father drink the liquor.

He believed that if you helped pay for it you could help drink it. We liked that part. We thought he was a fair man.

One time he took us over one of his women friends' house. It was the day after Christmas and every one was in the partying mood. He told us to act like we had some since and be on our best behavior. He went in first and left us in the car with a case of Rolling Rock beer. We were getting drunk just waiting on him. Slick asked me could I drive and I said that I could. He let me drive the car around the block. Well I really didn't know how to drive, I lied but I tried anyway. I turned the car out of the parking place and began to pull out when the car got caught onto the car in front of me and it started to grind and tear the car in front of me all up. I got so scarred and panicked and began to make it worst. Slick said put it in park and he jumped in the driver seat and pulled the car out and drove off as quickly as he could. It had snowed the day before and it was icy all over. But we got away and came back around the corner and parked in a different spot. All the time I'm trying to calm down. Well we drank about ten beers after that.

We looked up at the house and Papa sun was waving for us to come in the house. We got out and went in the house. When we got in there we were so surprised to see that his woman friend had five daughters. They were all lined up in the front room in front of the Christmas tree.

They were beautiful. They all were light skin with long pretty hair.
They stood like stair steps. We had one older and one younger than
we were. What more could two young boys ask for around Christmas
time. Papa sun told all of us to come into the dinning room and have
a toast. They passed around some eggnog around to us all and Slick
and mine was spiced. We got tore up that night. While we were having
a good time, Papa sun asked us why was his car parked in another
parking place. We was wondering how he knew. He said I always know
where my car is. He said which one of you little mother fuckers drove
my car. While we were taking our time trying to tell him the truth, he
just jumped on me and says I know it was your ass that was driving my
car. He talked about me all evening in front of all the girls. He did it
in a way that made me fill like a celebrity. I never had that much fun
all my life. It was so much fun seeing him make everybody laugh at my
expense. We all had a great Christmas holiday that year.

The more I hung out with Slick the more independent I became.
I knew how to make money. So you could not tell me too much and I
was legal. I became a hustler and I liked it to. I began to stay out late
and sometimes I did not come home. So I began to get into more and
more trouble at home. I felt that I was grown and no one was going
to tell me to stop doing what I wanted to. So I would get beat and put
on punishment. And my sister was the same way. They would put us
on punishment for weeks at a time. My stepfather was hanging around
some cops that were not always your stand up police officers. They
were getting high. They were smoking pot to. One day my sister and I
were sneaking around in their bedroom because we new we smelled pot
at night when they were in their room. We found where they stashed
their pot. We found what looked like an ounce of pot. We hit the
jackpot. We took a little and made it look like it hasn't been touched.
They had the best pot in the world. We shared some with our friends
and they thought we were the all that. The pot was so good we did
stuff to get on punishment. But I was tired of getting beat. I was at the
point in my life where I was going to stop people from beating on me
all together.

The word finally got out that we were getting high. People talk all
the time. Well we did not denigh it. We through it back at them that
they were getting high too.

They said you couldn't do what we do. Under our breath we said yes we could. They continued to get high and so did we. They would not let us get high in front of them but they new we did it. Sometimes when we were not on punishment we found their stash and stole some of their pot. They never confronted us about any missing.

My stepfather's friends would always come over the house after work with him to get high and drink, while they listened to his music. He had one of the best sound systems money can buy. He brought it from Vietnam. The system was made up of a turntable from technique, reel-to-reel tape deck, Panasonic stereo receiver and four technique speakers, and an eight-track player. The system was so awesome his friends thought he was the king of sounds. I thought he was the coolest man on earth. Nobody had a system like that. He was proud of it to. He also had one of the best album collections I ever did see; he had over a thousand albums.

His friends were over everyday.

They would get all highed up and would leave half of joints lying around. My sister and I had a ball when they left. He would be all drunk. He never knew a thing. He just thought we were getting better with our cleaning up. The drinking and drugging was getting very much out of hand. I saw it getting worst. But at the time I did not know what the effect it could have on everyone. I saw it before with my first stepfather and his family. But this progression of alcohol and drugs was different. It seems like they were doing it different.

But the insanity was the same. The parties got louder and the people got worst. They began to argue about all types of things. They would argue if the dog were black or white. Anything that sounds like a disagreement they were happy.

My mother decided to give Terry a birthday party. They said we could not come. We had to stay upstairs or spend the night over a friend house. We picked spending the night out. We were down the street at my sister's friend house. We saw who went in and out of the party. We would come in the house every now and then, until they would notice us and say get out. They were partying like it was the last party on earth. They had all the liquor, drugs, food you wanted. The best thing about it was they did not have to worry about the cops breaking the party up because everybody there was policemen, their wives and friends. They were having a ball. We were sitting on the steps outside about two or three houses down the street. When we heard about six guys come up to the house. We thought they were invited to the party. They asked if they could come to the party. My stepfather came to the door and told them that it was a private party and they were not invited. They left and did not sound like they were happy about not being able to go to the party. They continued to party, the music was playing loud and the people was having a good time. About twenty minutes went by and about twenty guys were coming up the street. As they walked by us they were saying we are going to get into that party.

My sister and I looked at each other and said, "We know they are not going to crash the party". We ran down the street to see what was going to happen. Our friends ran down the street with us. We knew that the party was full of cops. But those guys did not know it. They did not know what they were about to get in to. They were a gang from around the corner.

They went up to the door and knocked on the door. Terry came to the door and saw those guys out there and asked them what they wanted. They said we came to the party. Terry told them that he was sorry but it was a private party. They said move out of the way we are coming to the party any way. We looked with our mouths wide open. I said to my friends "are the crazy ". Do they know what they just did?

The guy that tried to push terry out of the way, was the first one to get grabbed. Terry grabbed him and took him into the party. While he was beating the guy up he was telling all the cops that these guys want to crash the party. All I saw were those guys running away from the house and every cop in the house was chasing someone. Then hell broke lose, every cop had someone in their hands and they were beating them like I have never seen before. They beat them boys down so bad I felt sorry for them, even though it was my house that they were trying to crash. The police car started to come and as they pulled up all of the cops pulled out their badges and shouted to them to lock all of them up. They were thronging them into vans like dead meat.

They had at lease ten vans. All of them were beat up and beat up bad. After all the police left and all the guys were locked up. All the police went back to the party. Now the party was different, everybody had a story. They all laughed and they began to drink more than they were drinking before. The party was on now. They even let my sister and me in. we were laughing and partying with them.

My mother walked in the room and she saw me put a joint to my mouth and everybody looked and she just waved her hand as if to say I give up. Then we all started to party like it was the last party on earth. The stories never stopped all night. I think I listened to every body stories; every one was so hyped up about the fight. They just could not stop talking about it. They pulled out all the drugs and liquor and everybody got tore up from the floor up. Next thing I new a lot of people left and others were all over the place, lying all on the floor and on the couches. When I looked up it was just my mother and me still woke. My mother looked at me and said come outside with me. We sat on the steps and watched the sun come up. It was a beautiful sunrise and a very nice morning. We sat there and smoked a joint and we both had our last drink. I felt like we had a bond that only a son and a mother could have. We talked about the drinking and the drugs. She told me that she would not ever do this again.

She looked at me and said "This was the last time we will ever do something like this" she said that this was not something she ever wanted to be doing with me or any of her children. She said that this was the first and the last party she will ever have like this. And we went on talking for a while and she stood up and said I love you I'm tired and we hugged I kissed her and she went up to her room and went to bed. I sat there and finished my drink, smoked the rest of my joint and watched the sun come up with one of the biggest smiles on my face. My mother and I out hung them all. And I was the last of the Mohicans.

This was the turning point in my life. I began to feel like a man. I felt like there was nothing that I could not do or accomplish. I was doing all the grown up things. I love to get high. I love the feeling it gave me. I was growing up and I loved it. Little did I know that this was the beginning of an addiction that would take me over in a way I could not imagine? It was the beginning of a ride only God could save me from.

CHAPTER 18

It's a Family Affair

Slick and I became an idle. We went everywhere together. All we wanted to do was make money and get high. I started smoking cigarettes too. Sly's father would take us to the bar with him and we would sit in the bar and drink with him and his friends. The first time he took in the bar with him, the bar tender told him, we were not allowed in the bar. Slick's pop said to him "who am I? I am Poppa sun and if I say I want my suns to drink with me, they are going to drink with me". The bar tender said then you guys would have to sit near the back. Poppa sun said I do not care where we sit as long as we get our drinks. After that day we were allowed to drink there as long as poppa sun was with us. We had so much fun. The ladies loved us and all of his friends did too. They all would come in the bar and buy us drinks and we would get tour-up we would be so drunk sometimes we could hardly stand up. But you dared not even look drunk in front of poppa sun. One night I was so drunk, I began to fall off the stool. Poppa sun saw me swaying at the bar stool and grabbed me and took me to the bathroom.

He said if I ever see you look like you are drunk again, I will beat the shit out of you. You will not make me look bad in front of my people. He said put your hand in your mouth and spit up. I put my hand down my thought and began to spit up. All of the liquor and food came out. He gave me a towel and said wipe your mouth and clean yourself up. I cleaned myself up and for some odd reason I felt a lot better. He said now when we go back out here you better act like you know. When I got back out there I sat up straight and I never looked drunk again in my whole life.

Slick and I continued to go to school and shine shoes after school, until the school went on strike the year of 1970. All the public schools in Philadelphia were on strike. And we loved it. We were out of school for three mouths. In those three months we shine shoes everyday. My mother and his mother let us do more or less what ever we wanted to do. Some times I would stay at his home and some times he stayed at mine. We kept our hustle and added a new one.

We had all the stores from 52nd and Walnut Street to 52nd and Market Street agree to pay us for cleaning the glass counter tops, wash their windows, clean the bathrooms and mop the floors. We had nine stores and made at lease seventy-five dollars a store. We would sleep all day and stay up all night if we did not have to work that day, at night we would walk the streets and go all over the city. The cops would stop us sometimes but most of the time they left us alone.

We walked everywhere all night long. We did not go to bed be until seven or eight in the morning. We walked everywhere all night long. We did not go to bed until seven or eight in the morning.

One evening we were walking through the University of Penn.'s campus and we walked into one of they're night classes. It was odd that they had a class that late at night. We went in any way. We sat in an auditorium with the professor down on the floor and we sat in the bleacher type setting and the room was round. It was about twenty-five people in the class. We just sat down and they did not take role call. The professor began to speak in a way that made every body feel so comfortable and calm. We looked at each other and smiled because we like how he began his class. He told everyone to take a deep breath and relax. He said that he was about to take us on a journey of the mind. He said sit back and enjoy the ride. At that moment we all relaxed and listened to him.

He spoke in a low whisper but for some reason we heard him very clearly. He said lets began our journey. I want you guys to build an office in your mind. The office must contain, a desk, a file cabinet and you must have two helpers. They can be who ever we want them to be and we can also make them up if we want to. So we began to imagine everything he told us to. He went on to say; now I want you to imagine an escalator and take it down one flight. Then take another one and take that one down another flight. Then he said take another escalate down one more flight. At the bottom of that escalator, he wanted us to imagine an elevator and imagine the doors opening. Then he said step into the elevator and push the button that said ten. He said that we are going down ten levels and at the bottom of that level he said the door will open and we should inter the room. The room will be empty and that is when he said that we needed to add our furniture. He said add your desk, and then add your file cabinets. He then said I will give you one minute to imagine who will be your helpers. Of course I picked two of the finest women that I could imagine. As soon as they appeared, they both walked up to me and said good evening Kevin and they both gave me a big kiss. I was in love with my office already. If he had not said another word I was in heaven. He interrupted us or at lease he interrupted me and said your time is up. You should have your two helpers, now lets move on to our journey. He said he want us to take some time to mess around in our offices, and do what ever we wanted to do.

I sat at my desk, in my big leather chair and told my helpers to get me some water and some food. As I sat there and eat my food I turned around in my chair and imagined a big picture window right behind my desk. I opened the window and flew out into the sky. It was a beautiful evening and for some odd reason I felt like flying. Well as I flew across the sky I looked down and I heard some people talking so I went closer and came down on the roof of this big house. As I sat on the roof, I looked into the window and there were some people in this very large front room. They were all from different ethnic groups. I liked seeing people from different races talking in the same room without a whole lot of chaos going on. I have seen racism on a few levels and it was a total turn off for me. Anyway while looking in the window the professor popped into my thoughts and said "I need you all to stop doing what ever you are doing and prepare to come back". Well I stood up and flew back to my office and flew into the window and landed in my chair. My helpers asked me did I have a good time on my flight and I answered and said that it was great; it was really nice of them to ask. The professor butted in again and told us to get back on the elevator and began to come up the ten levels that we went down. I kiss my two helpers and got on the elevator and pushed the button the read one. As the doors closed I waved at my helpers and they waved back. While going up those levels I was already planning on going back.

The professor instructed us to get off the elevator and get on the first escalator, then the second one and then the third one. As we were getting off the third escalator, he explained to us how this is a permanent room in our minds and we can always go back and do what ever we want to in our minds. Then he clarified what he meant and said we can do what ever we can imagine to do. He let us know that, if we can imagine it, we have the power now to manifest it. I really did not understand the value of that lesson until a few years later, when I was trying to study for a test. I first read the materials and then I called myself going to meditate on what I have read. As I began the process of my meditation, I decided to go down in my office and study with my two helpers, just as a joke. Well when I got down there, I began to tell the helpers all about the lesson that I was studying and they began to ask me questions about it and before I knew it we were having a great time. I told them that I had to go and I will return soon. We kissed and I came back up out of my office and out of my meditation. When I opened my eyes, it seemed like I was in a different place and time. I remember meditating for more than two hours. I did not think much of it until after I took the test and I got a (A) on the test. It kind of scared me because I had so much fun down there. I have a great time every time I return as well. I can live down there and do anything I want to do. But I have to remember that it's just my imagination and not the real world. It's a great place to go when you want to meditate.

After the professor brought us back, he dismissed the class and told us that we could come back to his next class. We ended up finishing the whole course and he really was a very deep person and a good professor. He taught us a lot about the psychology of human behavior as well as the different levels of our imagination. He explained how powerful the mind is and how to control it when it came to our imagination. During the semester he invited us to his home when he was having parties. We connected with a lot of the people in the class and he invited them as well. I guess he took a liking to us. We were very inquisitive and eager to learn. His parties were very strange but we had a lot of fun smoking his marijuana and drinking his wine. They began to get into chanting and things like that. They were doing telepathy and all types of things.

When they started chanting and ohmming we decided that we have seen enough. I believe they were getting into some kind of worshiping and we were not sure who or whom they were worshiping, so we took a few joints of marijuana and a bottle of wine and eased our way out the door and we never went back. They waved at us and said for us to take care and they said that they hoped to see us again. I can see in the professor's eyes, that he knew that it was a little beyond us. He gave me a look like take care and remember what I taught you because he knew that he may never see us again. It was a great lesson and experience that I will never forget. I never went to college but I feel like, I did take a psychology class at the University of Penn. And passed with a 3.9 GPA.

We were making so much money we did not know what to do with it. Slick knew an old lady name Miss Robinson. She liked Slick. She had this thing that she put to her throat to talk. She would speak in a very funny voice. One day she asked sly to come over her house. So we went over there. She said I like how you guys hustle. She said would you like to run a store? We said yes. She said I would put up the money for you guys to own your own business. We said great. She rented a storefront, on 56th and Spruce Street two doors from the corner. We went in there and cleaned the place up and painted it. It looked like a soda shop. Down the street from the store was an elementary school. So in the morning the kids would buy all kinds of candy and potato chips and stuff. We sold all types of stuff. We had cookies, candy, ice cream, and potato chips, pretzels and much more. You name it we sold it. It started to become a little hard in the beginning because we still had the window washing and the shoe shining to do.

So one day Slick would run the store and I would wash the windows and the next day we would switch. At night we both shine shoes.

Every night we would party with his sister and my sister. So we decided to get us an apartment. We got a friend of ours to rent us a room. The apartment was two blocks away from our store on 56th and Walnut Street. The party was on now. Every night after work we would go to our apartment. And get high.

His sister and my sister would get together and go to the apartment and get high. After we got high we would get the munchies and we would all go down to the store and make ice cream cones, candy and all types of stuff. This was happening every night. We started noticing that we were eating all our profits. The old lady would ask us how much did we make and we could never tell her a profit. She began to get suspicious and wonder why we were not making any money. Until one day we came to the store to open up and she was in the store. She had brought all of her fake jewelry and began to cook food in the store. She started taking over the store so she could see what we were doing. We were not having it, so we talked to her and told her that we were moving on and she agreed. It was fun while it lasted. We could not keep up with all the work we had anyway. It was a great experience and we could have been very successful if we were more serious about keeping the store. We were just a little immature about that level of business at that time.

Slick's family brought a house on 56th and Osage Avenue. We fixed the basement up and put a bar down there. We began to have parties, down there. With Slick having eleven brothers and sisters and all of their friends we had more than enough people for a party. His family was friends with the family on the next block, the Andersons and they had thirteen kids in their family. And they would come over with their friends. So we were always having a party. And everyone either drank or got high on something.

So the party was always happening. We stayed high all the time. We always had money so there was nothing stopping us from getting what we wanted. We partied all the time.

One night we went over to the Andersons house, just to see what was going on over there. Every one was home so when we got there, they said Tommie (Slick's brother) and them ware all up stairs. So we went upstairs to hang with the older guys. When we got upstairs we went into the middle to see if they were in there and when we opened the door. We saw Bobby, one of the middle Anderson brothers lying on the floor with a needle stuck in his arm.

We started hollering through out the house. Everyone came running to the room; they called the paramedics the tried to revive him and everything they could do. The whole house was in chaos. Everybody was running all over the house. Mom (Miss Anderson) was screaming and their father was going through changes to. They tried to keep mom calm down with no success. The paramedic came and tried to revive him and took him to the hospital.

Bobby died on the way to the hospital. And the whole house went crazy. Everyone was crying and morning like I have never saw before. Slick's sister was dating Bobby so that made it even more serious. Slick and I were just looking at everything going on. It was like we walked into the twilight zoon. We did not believe what we were seeing. It all started about seven or eight in the evening. All of the family members came over.

The cousins, nieces' nephews, aunts, uncles, and it seemed like all the friend of the family was there.

They finally got mom to lay down about two in the morning. The rest of the family started to calm down about three. Most of them went home but a lot of them were staying over. All the time Slick and I was just hanging around trying to support who we could and just be there for the family. Most of the guys all went in the middle room to lie down. So it was about four in the morning when Slick and I decided to leave and go take a walk. Slick went down the steps first.

Earlier it was talk that the guy who sold Bobby the drugs was mad because the cops were looking for him. And everybody thought he might come and start something so everybody was looking for him, just in case he wanted to start something. Well any way he never came around so everyone went to bed.

The whole house was quiet so we decided to leave. We were going down the steps and Slick thought he saw a man down at the bottom of the steps. He began to run back up the steps hollering that the man was down stairs. That woke everybody up. We ran up to the room where all the men were. We opened the door, shouting that the man was down stairs. We saw Tommie Slick's older brother with one leg out the window. When we opened the door shouting that the some man was down stairs, he jumped out the window from the second floor. We ran to the widow to catch him but he had already jumped out and hit the ground.

Everyone woke up and came running to the room and down the stairs. We changed from a man being down stairs to Ronnie jumped out the window. Everyone ran outside to see if Ronnie was all right. He had fell two stories and landed on his feet and broke his foot. He still got back up and ran across the street. We found him across the street next to a fire hydrant. They called the paramedics again. The paramedics came and took him to the hospital and we went with him. We stayed with him until they put a cast on him and sent him home. He said he wanted to go back to the Anderson. When we got back to the house everyone was still up and they all was made at Slick and me. Because they say we woke mom back up after they went through so much to get her to lie down. She was up in the room still crying when we got back. They asked us what man we saw. We told them that we thought we saw a man but it was a coat and a hat hanging up on the wall. They said if it was no for Tommie falling out the window they would kick our buts. So they made a decision to band us from the house until the funeral. We asked them, "We can not come back here until the funeral ". They said that's right, unless we want them to beat us up. We said we would stay away. All through the week we could come outside of the house but we could not come in. In 1971 Sly and the Family Stone a band, back then had a record out at the time called "It's a Family Affair" that record was played all that week. It was a very sad time back then. We all were very unhappy but for some odd reason it brought us together too.

Two families with over twenty-four siblings and me were trying to support each other. There was a lot of love during that time. It was the first time in my life that I felt so close to so many people. They accepted me as family.

The day of the funeral we all met up at the house. Everyone was there. All the family members and friends came out that day. Mom and Pop Anderson were leading the family with all the Carville's and me. They had a lot of cars loaded with people that day. It was one of the biggest funerals I have ever seen.

The funeral was really nice. It was so emotional. Every one was feeling the lost of bobby. The cars lined up around the block almost two times. After the funeral everyone was in a better mode. They all laughed at what went on the night bobby died. It was good that they got over it. Mom and Pop Anderson told them to leave us alone. They also said that we were allowed back in the house. That day it was a real family affair.

Speaking of an affair one of Slick's older sisters had her own apartment and Slick and I walked her home a few nights after the funeral, we stayed over that night but for some reason Slick left me there. When I woke in the middle of the night he was not there. His sister was still waked so we began to talk and get high. We smoked some joints and drank some beer. Next thing I knew we were making love. I felt like a man with her. She was my best friend's sister and she was older than me, what more can a young man ask for. Before that day she never gave me the time of day.

I was young and she was older. But I always admired her. She was cool and down to earth. This was a chance of a lifetime.

That morning my friend Slick shows back up and act as if he never left. His sister and I never said anything to anyone even up until this day. It was our secret. About three days went by and I began to fell a strange felling in my private area. I got scared it began to hurt every time I went to the bathroom. I did not know what to do. Nothing like this ever happened to me like this. All types of things were going through my mind. I did not know who to talk to. I was too ashamed to even talk to my friend Slick. I began to realize that I had a VD. Thank God they had some kind of sex education in school or I do not know what I would have done. So I decided to go to a community health center, in a neighborhood always across the city. I went to South Philadelphia.

I went into the center hoping and praying that what I had was curable. I did not want to die over a disease. I got in line and took a number. They call me after about a half hour. I went up to a desk and the lady asks me what I wanted. I said I wanted to see a doctor. She asks me what I wanted to see him for. I did not have a problem with her asking me that question but why did she have to ask me so loud. And when I tried to tell her she got to repeat what I said in a loud voice. I new dealing with her was not going to be an easy process. On top of that she had to repeat what I said, so I told her something was wrong with my private. Then she became a little quieter.

They made me wait for almost an hour and a haft before they called me back to see a doctor.

While waiting to see the doctor another nurse came in the room and asked me did I have sex with anyone. I told her yes. She wants her name and any information that I could give. I told them I did not know her address or phone number. She said ok and left the room. About a haft hour went by and the doctor walked in. as soon as I saw him I did not like him. He looked creepy. He looked like some kind of pervert or something. He asks me what was my problem and told him that my penis was hurting every time I went to the bathroom. He asked to take down my pants and let him take a look at my penis. I really did not want to show my penis to him because I did not like him. I pulled my pants down and showed him my penis he held it in his hand and some discharge was coming out at the same time.

He said I have to take a swab of this. To see what it was. So I said OK. He walks over to the counter and opens this jar that had some q-tips in it. They were the one sided tips and they were about six inches long. He walked back over to me and sat down in front of me. He takes my penis into his hand and as he began to insert the q-tip into my penis he started to say things like "people are out there doing all kinds of filthy things and nasty sexual acts, they need to go to hell" all the time he is pushing the long q-tip into my penis. At first I thought that the doctor had to go all the way up into your penis.

But then it began to hurt so much and he saying I have to dig all the way up there to get a good swab. I looked down and this man had haft of that q-tip up my penis and I began to scream and he stopped and pulled it out. I balled up my fist and looked at him and he backed up and said in a sarcastic manner "I had to dig deep to make sure I got a good sample. I looked at him and said right with my fist balled up. I was about to beat that doctor like I never beat anyone before. He did not come back, a nurse came in about a haft hour later and said you have gonorrhea and we have to give you a shot in your but. And we want you to take some pills. I said OK. She told me to bend over and she gave me a shot in the butt with a needle I have never seen before. It was long. She gave me a prescription and told me to not have sex for at lease two weeks after I finish all the pills. She was nice. It was at that point that I knew that the doctor was out to hurt me. I am still looking for him.

I went back to my friend's sister and told her what I had and she said that I must have given it to her because she knew she did not have anything. I told her she needed to get checked anyway. She went on as if what I told her was not important. I was just happy that I was cured. That is not a good feeling at all. Now we have two secrets.

CHAPTER 19

Splitting Up

The School strike went on for three mouths. From September to January we were out of school. Now the strike was about over and we had to go back to school. Slick and I were so involved with our hustle we did not want to give it up. By going back to school we could not do it the way we wanted to. I told Slick I had to go back to school and sly said he want to keep on hostelling. I was still at home with my mother and could not drop out of school. I was only thirteen years old. Slick were fourteen going on fifteen. He said that he was not going back to school. I asked him what he was going to do. He said that he was going to Washington D.C. with his father. He said that I could come with him. I thought about it for a while but I knew my mother would have given me hell. I really did not want to drop out of school anyway. I told Slick that I was going back to school. Slick said he was not going back. We made our decisions I was staying and he was going. So we got us a bottle of vodka and some weed and had a party just for us. We got drunk as two fish that night. The next day I went to the bus station with Slick to see him off. We promised to stay in touch and hugged. He got on the bus we waved and I went back home.

I felt like I had just lost my best friend and I did. For a couple of weeks nothing seemed the same. I stopped hustling and I did not have any money. I was going crazy, I always had money.

One day I saw an old man moving furniture. His name was Mr. John. I asked him did he need any help and he said yes. I helped him move the furniture and made forty dollars. I felt good and told him if he ever needed someone I will be available. Mr. John began to call on me every weekend and he gave me a regular job with him. Now things were staring to look up now. I was back at my hustle and keeping some money in my pockets. On day Mr. John got me a job working for some rich white man out in the sub burghs. He would pick me up at six in the morning and drop me off at the white man's house. And come back and pick me up in the evening. It was about six of us. We had to rake all his leaves into piles and bag them up. This man had a lot of land and we worked hard. The white man fed us lunch and gave us what ever we want to drink. He was a good man.

My mother was proud of me. She liked the idea that I was going to work at my age. She likes to see me being responsible, and handling my business. I did not ask her for anything. I brought my own clothes, shoes, and sneakers and had a bank account. For thirteen I was doing pretty well for myself.

One day I was downtown shopping and I met this girl name Wanda from North Philly. She was older than me. We began to talk and hit it off right from the start. After we finished shopping she asked me did I want to come over her house. I said yes. We went to her house. We talked for a long time. It was getting late and I had to go to work the next morning. Out of nowhere she asked me did I want to spend the night. I said that I would like to but I don't think my mother would let me spend the night out. She said have you ever spent the night out before. I said yes. She said so why would she say no now. I thought about it for a moment and said you got a point there. Wanda said did you ever spend the night out with other boys, why can't you spend the night over a girl's house? I said you are right I going to call and ask her. So I called my mother. I said hello mother, (her and Terry were in the bed sleep) she said yes baby what do you want. I said "mother can I spend the night out. "She said "where" I said over some girl's house. She woke right up then and said "what over some girl house?" and I said "yes". I said I am over a friend of mine house and she said I could spend the night. My mother said "No" you can't spend the night over some girls' house. I said why not you let me spend the night over a guy's house why not a girl. She said who is this girl? I said she is a friend of mine. She said where her parents are. I said she lives by herself. My mother went off then. She said no there would be no one home with you. She said "Hell no".

Then I herd Terry say what's going on and she told him that I wanted to spend the night over some girl's house and she lived by her self. Then Terry said let the boy stay he'll be all right. I could see the look on her face. She hesitated, everything got real quiet. I knew she was thinking and debating with herself and then my mother said go ahead but you better call me in the morning. And you know that you have to work in the morning. I said I know and I will call and I will go to work. She said ok see you tomorrow, then she said, "act like you know you hear me "and I said I will good night.

I hung up the phone and the girl said so what did she say. I said that she said yes. She said I told you she would let you. I said I don't believe it. She pulled out some weed and we began to get high. We went up stairs to her room and got more comfortable.

We began to make love and for the first time in my life, it was not forced on me or I was made to do it. It was real. It was all her and me. She made love to me, like I have never done before. Even up until today. Out of all the women I have been with, none of them ever made love like she did. She was so different from any woman I ever had. I was on her. Her back was flat on the bed. And while I was penetrating her, her hips were thrusting up in the air. I had to hold on to her so that she did not through me off her and the bed. The amazing thing about it was that her back never left the bed. Only her butt and hips moved. It was the most amazing love making I ever had.

Up until today no one has ever come close. We made love three times that night. And every time was better then the first. We woke up about five-thirty in the morning and made love one more time. Then I got washed up and kissed her good by and left. I got her phone number and told her I would call her after a got of work.

On my way home I had one of the biggest smiles on my face all the way home. I could not take it off. When I got home my mother was up waiting for me and when she saw my face she just said "men"

"I hope you had a good time" With a smile going around my head I said "I did".

This was the first time I had a normal sexual relationship. There was no dysfunction in it. There was no incest or any pressure. I made love and it was good. Even at that age I felt grown, mature, like a man. Out of all that it was ok with my mother. I needed the confirmation from her. Even though she was still young and needed some growing up to do herself. She still was the highaurcy in our family. She was queen bee. And we respected that.

I worked every weekend and spend the night over the girl house every weekend for about three mouths. We got along great until I went to see her onc Friday night. When I got there she came to the door and she had a black eye and a busted lip. I was shocked and asked her what had happened. She told me that her brother beat her up. And she said she had to move. Her brother was a very tuff guy.

He was one of them kind of guys that were always in trouble. She told me to stay out of it. I was only thirteen; it really was not much I could do. I wanted to help her but they both were older than me and he was older then her. She moved out of town and I did not see her again for almost four or five years. By that time I was a lot older and I was dating someone. That was another storey.

Well after she told me that she was leaving we went inside the house and started to get high. While we were sitting there her front door opened up and her brother came in. he ask her why was she still there. She said I going to leave when I am ready (in a very sarcastic voice). He said don't get smart I will punch you in the mouth again. Then he looked at me and said who the fuck is this? She said he my friend. He looked at me and said you better keep her in check. I just looked at him and didn't say a word. He stormed through the house and then he left. She said he just acting like he tuff. In the back of my mine he did look tuff. But somewhere in all that he respected me or at lease he gave me respect.

We went through our normal routine and got high and made love. It was a great night just like the other times. When I left we kissed and hugged and said our last goodbyes.

Now it seems like I lost two best friends but, I felt good that the separation was needed. I was still working on the weekends and going to school.

But the craziness in the house was getting worst. One night I came in from hanging out with some friends. And my mother, terry and terry's mother was drinking and listening to some records. Well they were having themselves a dandy good old time. I heard some arguing going on. I knew it was going to happen sooner or later. Well I went into the living room to see what they were arguing about. Well my mother want to play a record and terry's mother said that it was her turn to play what she was waiting to play. Well my mother said that she could hear her record after she play the record that she was getting ready to play. Terry's mother said oh no, you are going to play my record first. And they went back and forth.

Terry acting like a big kid put his hands over his ears. When his mother saw him do that she went off. She started calling my mother a selfish bitch and my mother called her a bitch and the fight was about to start.

My mother jumped up and terry's mother jumped up I jumped up and terry jumped up. Now we all were up and terry grabbed his mother and I grabbed my mother. They was hollering and screaming at each other. Terry shouted real loud and told them both to shut up and sit down. They both sat down very reluctantly. The good thing is that they did sit down. Well Terry was drunk and he was very mad. He said you all are fucking with my high. I am tired of you two going after each other. I will not choose between you two.

He told them that they were stupid to argue over some albums. He said some stupid ass albums. He said you all want to argue over albums. He yells at me saying "Kevin go get me some trash bags." I like when he gets drunk because he can get so stupid. So when he said go get some trash bags I ran because I knew what he was going to do. I brought him the trash bags.

He took them out of my hand and began to break every album he had. He had at lease two thousand albums. I stood there and watched him break each one. He looked up at me and said help me brake every last one of them. I had a smirk on my on my face because I did not want him to see me smiling. But I helped him break every last one of them. It took us about two and half hours.

His mother and my mother knew that he was just acting out; they knew he would regret it tomorrow when he sobers up. But they stood back and let him destroy all of them. I started out just braking of some of them with out any feelings. But after awhile I began to have fun. So I began to break them for real. He was sweating like a dog but he was determined to break all of them. After we finished he got up and went to bed. We put over twenty-five bags full of broken albums out for the trash. And I laughed all night. But deep down inside I was very disappointed in him for doing it. Just to prove a point that did not make any sense. He could have just told his mother to go home and shut down his system. But he was one of those type men. Who always have to over prove a point?

I was still doing any thing I wanted to do, staying out late, getting high and drinking. My sister and I were determined to do what we wanted to do. They were still putting us on punishment.

We stayed in our rooms for weeks at a time, and he was still beating me every time I did something. We were confined to our rooms. If we got caught out of our rooms we would get more time and I would get beat. I got to the pint where I could not take it any more. So I called a family meeting. My mother asked me what did I want to talk about I told her that I wanted all of us to be at the meeting. I had something that I wanted everyone in the family to know. She said I don't know what you are trying to do but it better be for a good reason. I told her that it was for a good reason. She just shook her head and went in another room, shaking her head.

That evening Terry came home, (my sister new what I was going to say) my sister ran to him and told him that we were having a family meeting. He went in the kitchen and got some ice and sat down in the living room and fixes himself a drink. When I came into the room he had this smirk on his face, that he always have when he was going to beat me. A look like (what do you have to say now?) look. He was all about philosophy and logic like Mr. Spook on Star Trek. He always tries to logically deal with us. I always asked him when logic don't work what do you do.

He would say logic always work. We just called him the logic nut, and the philosopher with no brains.

Well what I was about to say made a lot of sense to me and I was not going to back down from what I wanted. I did not know that I was about to go through my rights of passage, but something inside of me told me to make my stand. At thirteen I knew that this was the time for me to stop the insanity.

CHAPTER 20

Stop the Insanity

Everybody sat there and looked at me with this look on their faces, like what do you have to say. They knew I had a thing for controversy or debate. I began to tell them how tired I was and how I believed that if we were going to continue living together some changes had to be made. My mother said what kind of changes? I said every since we moved to Philadelphia I have been getting beat by some men other than my father. I told Terry please do not take what I am saying personally. But I have been beat for the last nine years. I am tired of getting beat. So I fell that you all need to come up with another form of punishment.

Terry out of nowhere shouts out "if you act up you will get your ass whipped". I said (trying to stay calm) did you hear what I just said. Why can't you come up with another form of punishment because beating is not going to work, because it's not working now? Terry said "it will work if I have to beat your ass all day" with a smirk on his face. This was funny to him but I was as serious as a heart attack. My mother saw the look on my face and she knew that I was not playing. She knew that I was serious. She also knew that terry was just as stubborn as I was. So she decides to break the meeting up. She said stop this "Kevin just stop and go outside or something".

I said mother I am not going to cry for nobody again. So it doesn't make any sense to beat me if I don't cry. Terry jumped in and said you will cry when I whip your ass. I said no I will not. He got loud and I got louder. My mother jumped between us and pushed me out the room and told me to go outside.

I left but on the way out I said I am not crying for you or anybody else, so you can beat me all you want. Terry's last words were "you will cry" and my last words were you would never make me cry again. You or anyone else will never make me cry again.

And I meant that.

All night I planed what I was going to do. The next morning I went to school. I met up with my liquor runner. He was only seventeen years old but he had a beard and a mustache. He looked like a grown man. When he goes to the liquor store for us they never card him.

I met up with him and about three other friends of mine. We got together and put our money together. We had enough for two gallons of wine. We went to the football field and sat up on the bleaches and drank our wine. Back then when we got drunk we would sing do-wop songs or fight. This day we just sang our songs. And got tour-up and sang our songs. After the wine was gone we all broke up and went back to school. I decided to go back to school drunk as a wine-o on skid row.

I sat in the hall way on the steps where every one walked buy and began to call every one names. I called them every word in the dirty dictionary. I talked about their mothers their fathers, sisters, brothers and everyone else in their families. I came up with some new words to. It got to be fun after a while. Then it got to the point when I could not stop. The drunkenness in me began to kick in and I became totally indecent in what I was saying. I began to call people things I never would believe came out of my mouth. But I could not stop. The teachers came by and I said it to them, the counselors, students, everyone. Then I looked up and two policemen were walking towards me. My mouth was running so much I could not stop and I began to call them names two. We had the same two policemen in our school. Their names were Wiggins and Pane. They looked at me and said this little motherfucker is drunk. They both grabbed me by the arms and carried me two the office. I was no bigger then a minute.

They pulled my records and said you are suspended and we are going to call your mother and tell her to come get you. They got her on the phone and told her what I did and they said since he do not live that far from the school they said they would keep me until I got sober and then they will send me home with a note on my chest. Just in case the police stopped me.

I sat in the office with Wiggins and Pane and they just laugh at me. They just could not understand why I would call all those people names as little as I was.

They said that I was lucky that some one did not kick my butt for all the names I called them.

I was still a little woozy and dizzy but I felt myself coming around. I was getting sober. I knew that I was going home soon and began to get prepared for that. They just did not know why I did what I did. I knew that I had to something big to get in trouble. I was about to meet someone and go to war. I had to get back into my war mode. It took all I had to get prepared for what I was about to confront. The war was on and I was going to the front line. The fight was on and I always was up for one. I never ran from one and I was not about to miss this one.

I am fighting for my dignity, my manhood and my sanity. Going through those beatings were starting to drive me crazy.

I am a warrior and I come to the war with a whole lot of gut and heart. So when you come to wars with me you better bring you lunch and your dinner because you are going to be there for a while. I don't give up and I don't retreat. I knew that he was coming with all he had and I was ready for what ever he had. It did not mater that he had been to the Vietnam War or that he was on the Philadelphia Police Department. I had thirteen years of hard knocks; I was already tired and beat up to the point where I was not taking it any more, so I say, bring it on.

The police officers and the principle of the school looked at me and said he look sober enough; they said we are going to send you home. Just for the fun of it they wrote a note and pinned it to my chest and sent me home. They called my mother and told her that I was on my way and for her to look out for me. I walked out the office with an escort of two policemen and some of the kids I cursed out, they wanted to see me get put out of the school. It was funny the way they walked me out. It looked like I was headed to death row or something. It looked like dead man walking. I had a smirk on my face, which I tried to hide. I wanted it to look like I was a hardened criminal or something. They walked me to the main entrance doors and pointed me in the direction of my home and told me to go straight home. They said that they would call to see if I made it there. They said if I do not go straight home they will call the police and have me picked up and taken to jail.

I began my walk home all the time thinking of the different ways of how this thing was going to play out. I wanted him to come to his senses but I knew that he was not that kind of creature. I just wanted the abuse to stop. I know that children needs to be punished and sometimes they need to get there buts beat. But in my case I have been beat unnaturally for the last nine years. I have been beat with belts, iron cords, whips, switches, punched, kicked, call every name in the book, told how low and filthy I am, told I will never amount to anything, attempted sexual abuse, and emotionally beat down,

And this went on almost everyday by my step father. And Terry started where he left off with the beatings. How much more can a child take? Don't get me wrong if it was not for the many times my mother told me how special I was, how proud of me and how smart she knew I was, she also would say stuff like you got a whole lot of since and stuff like that. I don't think I would be the man I am today. The things she said to me back then, keep me going strong, even up until today.

But let me reframe that statement about how much a child take can. I am a thirteen-year-old young man. I will not take another beating from any man. So what ever he's going to do will be the last time that I go through this with any one. The next time I get beat by any one will be because I'm in a fight and we will be getting it on and I will not be crying.

Well as I walk through Black Oak Park (now known as Malcolm X Park) I can see my house and in the door way my mother is standing there with her hands on her hips. As I walk pass tree by tree I can see her clearer and clearer. When I got to the edge of the park I can see her with this look of discuss on her face. At the edge of the park was 52nd street. My house is between Larchwood and Pine Street. On a little block called Addison St., my street was next to Osage Avenue, which also was a little street between Larchwood and Pine Street. And on Osage Avenue was Bell elementary school.

As I cross the street I can see tears in her eyes. I was not trying to hurt her; it had nothing to do with her. I had to keep in mine that I had to prove a point and I could not let any one or any thing get in the way of that. I knew that some one may get hurt but it was a chance I had to take. I knew that if anyone was going to get hurt out of this it was going to be me. And I say that literately. I am trying to prove a point and my life is at stake. I cannot go another day with someone beating on me as if I was someone's slave or punching bag. So we have to come together and solve this problem I have, by any means necessary.

The closer I get the worst I am feeling because I can not stand to see tears in my mother's eyes or to see her cry. I just can't stand it. Hear I am being the cause of it and I am not feeling to good about it right now. On top of what I know I am about to go through. These feeling are not what I bargained for. I am an emotional wreck right now and I do not know how to deal with them. Plus I am still a little drunk from all the wine I drank. Right now I am going through so many changes and I do not know how to sort it out. I figure I will just play it by ear, from this point on, because I don't know what else to do.

My house is the first house on the block. So as soon as I come on to the block the first house is right there. There she is standing in the doorway, looking down at me as I approach the steps.

I look up at her and she looks down at me and says "why why do you drink like that and why are you drinking in school?" for a lack of better words and not thinking what would be the best answer for that question and adding fuel to the fire I said "because I like it". Well that answer did not set to well with her and it only made her angrier. She gave me a look and as I proceeded to walk by her she brought her hand way behind her so that she could get a real good swing and whacked me upside the back of my head, with a force that pushed me through the second set of doors. She shouted at me to go to my room and don't come out ever. She had tears running down her face and that made me feel real bad about what I just did. I went to my room and sat on the bed and cried for about an hour. I did not know if I made the right decision about setting up this confrontation with Terry. The last person I wanted to hurt was her. I was confused and angry with my self. I wished I could take it all back.

But something in my mine and my spirit was telling me that I must go through with the plan. Something was telling me that this was me destiny. That this was the curse I must take. I settled down for a while after these thoughts were going through my mind. And then I just relaxed and lie down on the bed and put my hands behind my head and stared at the ceiling. I felt calm come over me. It was a spiritual feeling. I cannot explain it but something came over me that made me feel empowered with a calm relaxed feeling.

I was not afraid or I did not feel like he was a big deal. I felt like I could take what ever he dished out, without any fear. I knew that he was going to come in the room with stubbornness with a mission to make me cry no mater what it would take. He was the kind of man that could not deal with being wrong. He was the logic man and he was the philosopher. You could not tell him anything because he felt he was smarter then all of us put together. He talked that stuff to my mother but we never brought into it.

We knew things like Murphy's Law. That if it can go wrong it will go wrong. Be cause as we grew up we saw how bad it could get, so no one can tell me that everything's going to be all right and we all will live happily ever after. Be cause if something bad happens it could happen again. So the only thing you could do in life is to deal with ever comes down the pike. And try to keep your head in the mean time. Be cause if can happen it can happen. And the only thing that matters after that is how you deal with it. And my case this is how I am dealing with it. I am staying calm and keeping my mind at peace. Because if I start to worry about what he's going to do it will drive me crazy.

Lying there thinking about how I ended up in this room I began to laugh. I did believe that I got up that morning, met up with my friend, drank two gallons of wine, got drunk, sat in the middle of the school's hallway and call all those people names, got taken to the principle's office, almost locked up, suspended for a week and sent home with a note on my chest.

It all started at eight in the morning and it is two thirty in the after noon. In seven and a haft hour I have been through some trying things. And now I am facing a major beat down. Yes I was lying there laughing because I did not believe this day. I know that everyone at the school that knew me was gong to tell everyone what I did. I will hear that for a while. Kids that age would make me out to be cool or something. I did not do it for any recognition but you can't tell them that. As I lay there laughing about my day, the door opened and I knew that the laughing was over.

I looked up and Terry was standing over my bed with a belt in his hand and a smirk on his face. I did not have a problem with the belt (even though it was not your ordinary belt. It was one of those belts that the police use to hold all of their equipment on; it's called a "Sam Brown Belt". They are thick and heavy) I had a problem with the smirk on his face. Then I took a second look at the belt and I thought to myself he is really going way out with this beating. Hear I am weighing a good ninety pounds wet and he weighing at lease two hundred and twenty pounds standing six feet two inches and I am only five feet five and he needed to bring in the heavy artillery.

I just stood up and faced him and began to get myself physically prepared for what I knew was about to go down. I knew I was in for one of those old fashion beatings. When I say old fashion I mean old as in slavery old. He stood there and said "you just had to do something did ten you". I said "I told you, yawl need to come up with a new form of punishment because I am not going to cry for nobody beating on me again" I am tired of getting beat. With that same smirk on his face he says "and I told you that if you fuck up I will whip your ass and you will cry. And I said "no I won't" and he said, "well are you ready" and I said, "yea I'm ready are you ready" he said "you can take off those clothes" I took off all my clothes except for my underwear. He said you could take them off too. I looked at him dead in the eye and I took off my underwear.

Now I was naked and I really felt like a slave being degraded and hillmiliated. But I stood there like a man a I looked him in the eyes and he said "are you ready and I said "yes are you ready" and he said "yea I'm ready" he look at me and I look at him and he began to swing that big black belt. He began to beat me every place he could find open. I tried to block as much as I could but he was getting the best of me. As he beat I just looked him in the eye I did not make a sound and I did not shed a tear. He brought the belt from every direction he could. He was huffing and puffing but he was determined not to stop until he saw a tear come from my face.

I was determined to not give him what he wanted. I just looked him in the eyes so that there would be no mistake if he saw a tear or not. This battle or shell I say beating went on for a half hour and I could see that he was getting tire. But he was determined to break me and I was determined not to be broken. He was sweating like I never seen before and I started to see blood squirting from my skin. Whelps were starting to form all over my body but I couldn't be concerned about that I just had to keep my focus on him. I just kept looking him in the eyes.

This went on for another fifteen minutes and then it happened as I was looking him in the eyes something so profound happened for one moment he was looking me back in my eyes and all of a sudden his whole domineer changed. That look of determination was no longed there. I saw a sudden look of shame, like I have never seen before on any ones face. All I could think of was that he was thinking, what was he trying to do, how far was he determined to go, to make this thirteen year old boy cry. When he noticed that I saw the look on his face, I could tell he knew that I knew what he was thing. Then he stopped he was huffing and puffing and could not hardly talk, but he said in a very tired voice, "I'm not going to kill you" and walked out of the room.

I stood there for a minute and looked over my body and blood was coming out of eighty-five percent of my body. I was shocked I did not know that he was tearing the skin off me. I did not know that I was bleeding that much. Now the look of my body made me cry. I knew he was going to try his best to make me cry but I did not know how much or how far he was going to go.

My mine told me to block out everything. I must have been in a very deep state of mine. Because if I was conscious of the beating I took, I believe I would have gone crazy or something if I were fully conscious. I did not feel any pain at that time. I was hurt and my mine would not let me feel the pain or fully notice the blood, right away. So I just lay on the bed, cured up and cried. My cry was more of happiness than for the pain. I felt good that I did not quit, I did not give in. and most of all he could not beat me and I could take what he did to me. The war was over and I beat it fear and square. I am a soldier, yes a little wounded but there are always some injuries in war, but I feel I came out better that he did. My body will heal but his mentality my take awhile. I hope he can recover from what he put us through. It was good that I stood my ground and I prove my point that I will not cry, for no one again.

CHAPTER 20

Right of Passage

As l is lying there wondering how was I going to take care of all the wounds that I incurred, I did not know where to begin. It never crossed my mine what my mother would think.

After any one of us would get beatings, some one would always come in to make sure that we were ok. I knew that one of my sisters would be knocking at the door at any time so I just lay there and next thing I knew, I must have fell to sleep.

As I dreamed I could hear someone screaming and crying. They started to scream louder and louder. I was deep in my dream at the time but the screams became so loud that I opened my eyes and seeing my mother screaming with her hands over her mouth startled me. I attempted to jump up but my sister was holding me down. She was crying and she would not let me up. She just kept crying and saying stay still.

I did not know that the sheets that I had wrapped around me had stuck to the blood that had dried on my body. My mother was in total shock. She just stood there crying and saying how she did not know that he would beat me that bad.

I was in total shock because I could not stand to see my mother or my sisters cry like that. They were crying as if I was going to dye. I just did not see what they saw. Because I was out of touch with the whole beating I did not see every thing.

When I took a good look at my body, I had whelps all over my body and all of them were bleeding. The sheet that covered me, looked like I had at lease two or three gallons of blood pored on me. When I looked down at the sheets I did not see any white parts of the sheet. It looked like I was in a pool of blood. The blood had dried and the sheet was sticking to my skin. My sister was trying to take the sheet off my skin without reopening the wounds. But every time she tried to pull on them I hollered. I did not know that taking those sheets off was going to be that hard. If I knew I would have laid there naked. My mother said, "Stop pulling on those sheets". She said to my sister "run him some warm water". She said get my first aid kit out of my closet. She told me to get up off that bed before I got stuck to it.

After my sister ran the water my mother told me to get into the tub with the sheet on. Once I got into the water and soaked for a while, the sheet came right off. She told me to give her the sheet. I said mother I will be naked; she gave me that look and said, "Boy you don't have anything that I have not seen before".

She began to clean my wounds and the dried up blood from my body. While she was doing it, I could tell she was into deep thought. I could tell that she was going to do something. I could tell that it was not going to be something violent. But she knew she had to make some kind of decision. I just let her wash me and think to herself. As she washed me I was doing some thinking myself.

I was thinking that now that I am not going too get beat anymore, what would be their new form of punishment. Would they try to lock me up in my room? No, that will not work. Will they take stuff away from me? No that will not work because I don't have any thing that I care about and they know that. So what will it be I wondered? Then I started thinking that she might get rid of one of us. She might kick me out of the house. She may tell me that I have to go. Then again she may kick him out for beating me so bad. She might kick both of us out. But then I got to thinking it took her a long time to find a man, which was haft way decent. And except for his drinking and beating on me, he was not that bad. All kind of things was running through my head and I was trying to sort out the best scenario. I found myself thinking like Terry. I was trying to figure out the most logical decision that she could make. I started to laugh to myself.

While I was in deep thought my mother was telling me to get out of the tub. She took the towel and patted me down real softly and led me to my room. My sister had changed the sheets and cleaned up my room.

My mother rubbed some ointment on my wounds and told me to let the wounds air dry for a while. And try not to wipe the ointment off for a while. She said you have been punished enough so just stay in your room today and get some rest. And we all will talk tomorrow. She let my sister bring in a TV, so that I could watch some TV. She also sent my sister to the store to get me something to eat. And she kissed me and left the room. I could still see the tears in her eyes. I knew she was hearting and all I could do was just let her be for the time being.

I began to fell guilty. I felt that I had started something deeper then I had anticipated. I knew that what went down was very serious and that some deep changes were about to happen. I just did not know the magnitude of the changes. My mother was going to do something deep and it was going to affect everyone. I just watched TV and put it out of my mine. This was a golden opportunity to lay back, eat and watch TV in my bedroom for a while and I was going to take advantage of it. I was out of school for a week and I did not have anything to do, until the weekend when I went to work. So I was taking full advantage of this newfound opportunity. I just might milk it a little. I might play my sympathy card. I will see in a couple of days.

I thought we were going to have a meeting the next day but everybody went about his or her way as if nothing happened. They just were not saying anything. The first day I did not care because I was enjoying my newfound freedom and I was never so sore all over my body. The whelps were beginning to scab and the bleeding stopped. I knew I was not going anywhere that day.

The second day I just let it go by. Nothing was going on. Nobody came to my room or asked me were I all right. The day went on without any communication from any one. I went down stairs and fix me something to eat and got something to drink. The whole day went by and I basically had the house to myself. Then the third day I started to wonder why no one was saying anything. It seemed like no one wanted to bring up the subject. My mother was quiet and just did not say anything more then, how are you feeling and stuff like that? My sisters were the same. I started to think that I hurt everyone. But they would ask me if I needed anything and stuff like that. So I knew that they were not mad at me.

I could still see the sadness and hurt in their eyes and I did not want to bring the subject up. Deep down inside I still wanted to know what was going on. Then I notice that I did not see much of Terry. I wondered where he had been. I have not seen him since we had our confrontation. I started to wonder if he had moved out and that was the reason why no one was saying any thing.

I decided not to say anything until some one mentioned it. I was not going to push the issue. I decided to enjoy the rest of my vacation. Things went on that way for a while and I did not say anything. Then out of nowhere my mother calls me from down stairs to come out of my room. I answered her and she said would I please come down stairs. I got up and went down stairs. I walked into the living room and to my surprise Terry, my sisters and my mother was sitting down, waiting on me. This was the first time I saw Terry since our confrontation. They asked me to have a seat. So I sat down. My mother began to speak. She said, "We got married and brought this house, so that we all could be a family. We have tried to give you all what ever we could. We did the best we could in trying to discipline you and keep you on the right track. We tried our best in raising you all. Since we have been together it has always been something going on. We have been fighting about going to bed, staying out late, coming in on time, all kinds of things. We have tried to get you all to clean your rooms, and keeping this house clean. It is always a fight. We are tired of trying to make you all grow up. We have come to the understanding that you are already grown, and no matter how long we try to make you grow up to our standards you will all ways fight us. So we have come to the conclusion that you all are already grown. And there is nothing more we can teach you.

So we have decided to move out and leave you the house and all that goes along with it. We have rented an apartment and will be moving out. You all act too grown for us. So we are giving, you all, the house and everything in it. You can have all the furniture and everything else. You have to pay all the bills. We hope that with your entire grown up ness, you all can maintain this house, and if you can't make it on your own, you will have to find your way in the world. You all will not be able to come live with us. So if you fell to make it out hear on your own we will be available to give you some advice and that's all.

We all looked at each other. It took about five or ten minutes to sink in but when it did we all jumped up and said "yes that's what we want to."

They said that they will pay the next mouths mortgage, electric, gas and water. After that we had to keep up the rest of the bills forever. We knew we were all that, and we knew we could handle it. My oldest sister had a job and I had my part time job and I knew that I could get a better job or I can hustle more. M y next to the oldest sister said that she felt that she could get a job too.

My youngest sister was still two young but we told my mother we would look out for her. We told my mother that we could handle the house and for her not to worry.

We were used to living on our own, from the past. We lived for two years at the other house. So we felt that it would not be a problem doing it again. Plus we are a little older now. We new that we could handle it, and even if we didn't we wanted to try it. We did not want to be told what to do. We did not want anyone to tell us when or what time we had to do something. We were not used to being told what to do. I believe that's where my unwillingness to listen to authority comes from. It is a bad habit that I believe began back around that time in my life. But never the less this was the time in my life that I became a thirteen-year-old king.

Now I could be my own man, do my own thing and live my life the way I want to live it. That's where my hard headedness began. No one was able to tell me anything no more. That's when I believe I began to raise myself. At thirteen I have seen death, I have owned my own business, I new how to make money and I knew how to make love. What more did I need to know. I was the youngest man I knew. And now I was joint owner of a house. You could not tell me anything.

My other and Terry moved out and by the end of the week I was a grown man. When I went back to school I went in as a crown-up not a child. My whole demeanor was different. I walked different, talked different and acted different. I was determined to do all the grown things. I did well for a long time. Some teachers asked me was everything all right? They saw a difference in me.

Don't get me wrong I was still doing some things that I was not supposed to be doing. Getting high was the thing to do. I came up in the seventies. In the seventies getting high and chasing girls and listening to music were the things to do. I loved it. You could not tell me anything at that time in my life. I never felt freer.

This was the first time in my life that there were no chains or restrictions holding me back from doing anything I wanted to do. Even though today I wish I had some chains. Having no chains for any young man is not a good thing. I look at some of the plight in the black community today with the lack of male role models and just the lack of discipline that gives a young man the idea that they can do anything that they want to do and that's not a good thing.

This is the when I began to realize that I had to be my own father. All I knew was I did not want to be like any of the ones that were in my pass. So I decided to be the opposite of the ones I knew. That was my philosophy at the time. It helped, but I needed a whole lot more. I just entered the school of hard knocks. I prayed and asked for guidance because I knew that I had no ideal which way to go.

This was only the beginning of "Raised by a Nine Year Old (King)".

ABOUT THE AUTHOR

Heaven HI, my name is Hezekiah Nevels author of "Raised by a Nine Year Old King" Please do not feel sad for that young boy or the man that he became. We go through things in life for a reason. It was those things that made me the man that I am today. I am a very loving, caring, sensitive, strong, humble, down to earth man of God with a high level of a sense of humor. So please don't feel sad for me.

I learned that in order for me to recover from all the trama and drama that I was put through, I had to go throgh a process of forgiveness and restoration. I had to learn how to forgive and how to restore that person back to when I loved, liked or just new them. When you restore someone, you forget every thing that they did wrong to you and all you remember about them is when you did not have a problem with them. Most people can forgrive but they do not know how to restore. What happens when you can't restore, is you can't forget and if you can not forget you will not be able to fully forgive. Like I said its a process.

Today I am a very susessful businessman. I own a General Contracting company and I am a Green Job Training Instructor in my own training center. I learned that, why give a man a fish sandwich, to eat for today, when I can teach him how to fish for life.

I encourage you to read the following series to hear about the life of this young boy and how he taught me how to be the man that I am today. Through trail and era he rose about his situation.

The two things that I'm most proud of is that through all that I went through, I never spent one night in any prison or any hospital. For that I am truly blessed. So many of our tramatized brothers and sisters end up in Jail, instututions or death. I was given favor.

Thank you.

Hezekiah Nevels

So the Saga begins.
Look out for Volume Two
"The Life of A Thirteen Year Old"
Growing Up In the Streets of
Philadelphia.